THE DEVELOPMENT OF
LINGUISTIC SKILL IN TWINS, SINGLETONS
WITH SIBLINGS, AND ONLY CHILDREN
FROM AGE FIVE TO TEN YEARS

UNIVERSITY OF MINNESOTA
THE INSTITUTE OF CHILD WELFARE
MONOGRAPH SERIES NO. XIV

The Development of
Linguistic Skill in Twins, Singletons
with Siblings, and Only Children
from Age Five to Ten Years

BY

EDITH A. DAVIS, Ph.D.

LECTURER IN PARENT EDUCATION
INSTITUTE OF CHILD WELFARE
UNIVERSITY OF MINNESOTA

GREENWOOD PRESS, PUBLISHERS
WESTPORT, CONNECTICUT

Library of Congress Cataloging in Publication Data

Davis, Edith Atwood, 1890-
   The development of linguistic skill in twins, singletons with siblings, and only children from age five to
ten years.

   Modified form of the author's thesis, University of
Minnesota, 1936.
   Reprint of the ed. published by the University of
Minnesota Press, Minneapolis, which was issued as no. 14
of the Monograph series of the Institute of Child Welfare,
University of Minnesota.
   Bibliography: p.
   Includes index.
   1. Children--Language. 2. Child study. 3. Psychol-
ogy, Physiological. 4. Twins. I. Title: The develop-
ment of linquistic skill in twins ... II. Series:
Minnesota. University. Institute of Child Development
and Welfare. Monograph series ; no. 14.
LB1139.L3D28 1975   372.6'01'9   72-141543
ISBN 0-8371-5890-7

Originally published in 1937 by the University of Minnesota
Press, Minneapolis

Reprinted with the permission of the University of Minnesota
Press

Reprinted by Greenwood Press, Inc.

First Greenwood reprinting 1975
Second Greenwood reprinting 1977

Library of Congress catalog card number 72-141543

ISBN 0-8371-5890-7

Printed in the United States of America

FOREWORD

Of all the developmental processes, symbolic behavior has held the interest of more investigators than any other. One of the early projects of the Institute of Child Welfare resulted in the McCarthy study, which described in detail the development of language in young children. The Day study, which showed the nature and extent of linguistic retardation in young twins, soon followed. In the present study Davis determines whether or not this retardation continues after the twin moves into the highly socialized environment of the school and whether or not only children actually respond to an environment that intrinsically seems especially favorable to more rapid language development. McCarthy and Day were concerned primarily with the content, form, and structure of language. Davis has added a study of articulation which shows that the mechanisms of expression follow a somewhat different developmental course than does language content. McCarthy and Day studied children from 1½ to 5 years; Davis studies children from 5½ to 9½ years. Thus out of this early Institute project, over a period of some years, there have come three interrelated studies which outline with some completeness the development of language from 1½ to 9½ years. Each study also has resulted in a number of incidental and associated studies.

Several points made in this monograph merit special attention. The linguistic retardation characteristic of twins, as found by Day, persists up to 9½ years, but grows less marked with increasing age. It is more marked in articulation than in language content. Only children at each age level are definitely superior. Also of interest are the wide individual variations found in the mastery of language among the 436 children observed by Davis. Some of the youngest children exceeded the performance of some of the oldest ones, and several of the 5½-year-old children who were in kindergarten exceeded the mean performance of 9½-year-olds in the fourth grade. While there was much overlapping, when comparisons were based on sex, occupational status, and intelligence, the group differences were clear cut, and gave a slight superiority to girls over boys, to the upper socio-economic groups over the lower, and to the more intelligent children over the less intelligent. These findings confirm those of McCarthy and Day.

Mrs. Davis is to be complimented on the ingenuity and thoroughness with which she has analyzed her data and on the insight shown in its interpretation. Her study will be read by students and workers in the field of child development for many years.

JOHN E. ANDERSON
Director, Institute of Child Welfare
University of Minnesota

ACKNOWLEDGMENTS

To Dr. John E. Anderson and to Dr. Florence L. Goodenough of the Institute of Child Welfare of the University of Minnesota I wish to express my gratitude for their interest, advice, and encouragement, without which this investigation could hardly have been brought to a conclusion.

I am deeply indebted to Miss Prudence Cutright of the Curriculum Department of the Minneapolis Public Schools, and to the late Dr. L. L. Everly, director of research in the St. Paul Public Schools, for permission to conduct this investigation in the schools and for access to records which in many ways facilitated the selection of cases and the interpretation of findings. I regret that it is impossible to make individual mention of the many officials and teachers who assisted me in locating subjects and arranging time and space for interviews. Welcome, interest, and cooperation were the rule in both public and parochial systems. A list of all the schools from which subjects were drawn is given in the Appendix.

Thanks are also due Dr. Ella J. Day for access to her original data on the language development of preschool twins. Finally, I express my gratitude to my husband, Dr. Ralph E. Davis, for his unfailing understanding and sympathy.

E. A. D.

CONTENTS

ix

THE DEVELOPMENT OF
LINGUISTIC SKILL IN TWINS, SINGLETONS
WITH SIBLINGS, AND ONLY CHILDREN
FROM AGE FIVE TO TEN YEARS

I. INTRODUCTION AND REVIEW OF RECENT STUDIES

PURPOSE OF THE INVESTIGATION

When Day (31) found that the language performance of her eighty sets of preschool twins fell far below the norms set up by McCarthy (80), further research into the comparative linguistic development of twins and singletons became imperative. Since both the Day and McCarthy studies stopped just before the age at which school experience usually begins, a supplementary investigation would logically start where the earlier ones left off. To avoid the complications which must result if school as a factor were ignored, it was decided for the present study to capitalize the common factor of school experience and carry on the research entirely in school buildings and during school hours, thus saving much time and securing better standardized working conditions than could be had in the home.

To obviate the possibility of the personal equation operating to intensify or obscure obtained differences between the groups to be compared, it was decided that the entire problem should be handled by a single investigator. The study was undertaken with the knowledge that the results might be entirely negative as concerns differences between twins and singletons, but with the conviction that in any case worth-while returns were assured from intensive investigation into phases of the use of language by school children that have been largely neglected in the past. To carry a little further the history of language development in twins and other children is the purpose of this investigation.

SUMMARY OF RECENT CONTRIBUTIONS IN THE GENERAL FIELD

Because of the widely divergent aspects of language development which have been investigated in the course of this study, only the literature dealing with the more general phases of the subject will be reviewed here. Since familiarity on the part of the reader with the McCarthy and Day studies is fundamental to an understanding of the techniques and objectives of the present investigation, no attempt has been made to duplicate the comprehensive reviews prepared by those workers.* Previous investigations in each special field will be discussed in the following chapters.

There have been no radical departures as to method, or major contributions as to content, in the study of language development since McCarthy's normative investigation (80). Recording by a stenographer has been utilized by a number of investigators (36, 111), and there have been attempts at perfecting a system of mechanical recording (152). Wellman and her associates (149) have made a careful analysis of the speech sounds of young children; Sommers (127) and Springob (128) have shown that corrective measures can improve articulation during the preschool period. Betzner's (8) elaborate investigation into the voluntary oral compositions dictated by pupils in the early grades indicates that children vary widely in their choice of themes, prefer the narrative to the descriptive and the realistic to the imaginary treatment, tend to bring their stories to a definite conclusion, and possess ability far in excess of the standards laid down by writers of elementary language textbooks. McCarthy (79) and Smith (125) have found that responses vary somewhat in length, structure, and function in different experimental situations. Piaget's influence (102) is seen in the conduct and interpretation of many investigations (1, 36, 59, 65, 123, 146). Smith (124, 126) has studied the effect of bilingualism on language development. McConnon (81) has demonstrated that the high reliability of the McCarthy technique "does not necessarily imply consistency over a period of time," and that "to obtain a stable index of a child's language responses it is necessary to take a number of samples in a number of situations." Much emphasis has been placed upon language as an index of social and personality development (36, 57, 65, 74, 84, 111). LaBrant (69) has attempted to use the clause as a unit of measurement.

The language development of twins has received little attention since the completion of Day's study, although Howard (55) found triplets similarly retarded. The measurement of resemblance in twins and siblings in physical, mental, and personality traits has been undertaken by Hirsch (51), Bakwin (5), Burks and Tolman (19), and a number of others. Newman (91) has continued to collect data on identical twins reared apart. Several investigators have been concerned with methods of determining identity (28, 108).

* For detailed summaries of the literature on multiple births see the Ph. D. dissertations by Ella J. Day (1932) and Ruth Howard (1934) on file in the University of Minnesota Library. Language development is adequately reviewed in the article by Dorothea McCarthy in C. Murchison, ed., *Handbook of Child Psychology* (2d edition, Clark University Press, 1933), pp. 329–71.

Perhaps the most stimulating work is that of Jones and Wilson (63), who have produced evidence indicating that identity per se operates to increase the similarity of those alike in appearance and the dissimilarity of those unlike.

The present is the first language study in which the only child has been treated as a separate entity. Unless our present way of life has produced a generation of only children markedly different from the previous one, Kolrausche (68), Bohannon (14, 15), and Friedjung (37), by concluding that only children are poorly adjusted in school and in their social relationships, painted a picture which is a gross caricature of the truth. Blatz and Bott (11) in 1927 found that only children had the best records in the behavior traits studied, and Goodenough and Leahy (44) did not obtain for only children an unduly high rating for undesirable traits of personality according to Blanton's scales. * Fenton (35) in 1928 was the first definitely to challenge the general view that only children have undesirable traits in a high degree, basing his conclusions on teachers' ratings by the Blanton scale on some two hundred young school children. Guilford and Worcester (47) substantiated his findings, while Hooker (52), by pairing 30 only children with children with siblings on the basis of school grades, sex, age, nationality, family organization, and IQ, found the only children better adjusted. Studies based on clinical material still show the only child in an unfavorable light, but until there are uniform methods for selecting cases these findings must be considered not proved.†

Higher intelligence in only children has been noted by Hirsch (50), Guilford and Worcester (47), Sutherland and Thompson (137), and Lentz (72), but in none of these studies were the cases selected in accordance with a cross-section of the population; hence it is extremely probable that the apparent superiority results from the inclusion of an unduly large percentage of children from the upper social levels, in which one-child families are more common. The question of only-child intelligence is involved with the birth-order controversy, for the reason that all oldest children have passed through a period of being only children, and the definition of an only child varies with the individual investigator. Hsaio (56) found no difference in intelligence between the first- and second-born, but Maller (83) found the mean intelligence of only children to be slightly below that of children with one or two siblings. Commins

---

* Devised by Dr. Smiley Blanton. See his *Child Guidance* (Century Co., New York, 1927), pp. 242–87.

† Several minor studies of this type are described in G. and L. B. Murphy, *Experimental Social Psychology* (Harper's, New York, 1931), pp. 345–52.

(24), Steckel (130), Thurstone and Jenkins (141), and Arthur (3) have produced evidence indicating higher intelligence in the later-born of a family, but Jones (62) concludes after a thorough review of the literature that "intelligence is not yet proved to be a variant with order of birth."

Although there is a popular belief that the younger siblings in a family have an advantage in the acquisition of language, such quantitative evidence as we have points toward superiority of the only child, and as many of the early biographical reports indicate an advantage for the first-born as for the later-born. Markey (84) with charming naïveté reflects the prevailing attitude when he discusses the case of an only child whose speech development was so slow that meaningful words were not used until 24 months. This child, he says, generally played alone while at home, and "this would tend to retard speech development" (page 95).

One reason for the inclusion of a group of only children in the present study was McCarthy's (80) discovery of the linguistic superiority of those children who spent much time with adults. Since the data were collected, rather startling confirmation of the findings of the present study has appeared in the work of Levy (74), although his method of selecting cases probably invalidates some of his conclusions. From several hundred clinical cases of "overprotection" he selected 20 which in the opinions of lay observers and professional workers were "pure" cases of "maternal overprotection." These children (apparently all boys) tended to show superiority in vocabulary and all phases of verbal ability, but to be only at grade, or even retarded, in arithmetic. Levy concludes that when an overprotected child enters the first grade his initial linguistic advantage facilitates his learning to read, but when he encounters arithmetic he is on a par with other children. The characteristic reaction of the overprotected is to become more and more interested in the subject in which he is favored, to the neglect of the subject in which he has no advantage, thus increasing the discrepancy. Although Levy's findings can hardly be taken at their face value, they suggest a fruitful field for further investigation.

The whole question of personality adjustment in the only child has been ably reviewed by Campbell (20), who concludes that the presence or absence of siblings is not of crucial importance in the development of personality. It would seem, however, that until our knowledge is more extended than at present, the sibling relationship is a factor which should be considered in setting up certain types of experiments with children.

II. METHOD OF INVESTIGATION

SELECTION OF CASES

It was apparent from the start that if this investigation were to yield results at all conclusive, a large number of cases would be necessary. Both twins and singletons must be representative of the Minneapolis and St. Paul population in socio-economic status; there must be equal numbers of boys and girls; and enough age levels must be studied to show development. Furthermore, since Mc-Carthy found superior language development in preschool children who spent much time with adults, and since the inclusion of such children in her study might have accounted in part for the difference between her subjects and those of Day, it was decided to select a group of only children at each age to compare with the twins and with the ordinary singletons with siblings.* The twins studied must not only be equally divided between the two sexes, but must approximate the occurrence in the general population of fraternal and identical like-sex pairs and of unlike-sex pairs.

Because the method devised by McCarthy and employed by Day had to be gradually extended for use with older children, and because a difference between twins and other children at the age of 4½ years had been established, the logical age at which to begin the collection of data seemed to be 5½ years. Most children in Minneapolis enter kindergarten soon after the fifth birthday, and by the age of 5½ have had time to become adjusted to the change from home to school. Nevertheless, early in the investigation it became apparent that in at least one phase of the problem of language development, that of articulation, the kindergarten year is extremely critical. Such wide variation in speech ability occurred among kindergarten children that only a very large group could be depended upon to give a sampling adequate for all the contemplated inter-group comparisons.

The final procedure was to concentrate the study at the 5½-year level. Since the transition from kindergarten to first grade, although less of an ordeal now than formerly, is still a milestone in the

---

* For purposes of convenience, singletons with siblings have been referred to simply as "singletons" throughout the study, while singletons without siblings have been called "only children."

child's life, a small group of cases at 6½ were selected, but no further study of yearly changes was attempted. The final group was 9½ years old, at which age most children are to be found in the second half of the fourth grade. By this time they have had a considerable amount of training and practice in oral expression yet remain cooperative and easily interested in a simple experimental situation.

The location of suitable sets of twins was greatly facilitated by the use of school registration cards, which give exact age, school history, and paternal occupation. Information as to the presence of other children in the home was obtained from teachers, nurses' records,

TABLE 1. — DISTRIBUTION OF CASES BY AGE, SEX, AND SIBLING RELATIONSHIP

AGE IN YEARS	TWINS			SINGLETONS			ONLY CHILDREN			ALL		
	Boys	Girls	Both	Boys	Girls	Both	Boys	Girls	Both	Boys	Girls	Both
5½.	48	48	96	49	50	99	27	26	53	124	124	248
6½.	11	11	22	11	11	22	10	9	19	32	31	63
9½.	24	24	48	26	26	52	12	13	25	62	63	125
Total. . .	83	83	166	86	87	173	49	48	97	218	218	436

the children themselves, and when necessary by home visits. There were non-only singletons galore from all occupational groups, but only children from the lower occupational groups proved surprisingly difficult to find. Since the study of only children was subsidiary to the main problem, the number of only children was finally made

TABLE 2. — DISTRIBUTION OF SETS OF TWINS BY AGE AND SEX

Age in Years	Both Boys	Both Girls	Unlike Sex
5½	18	18	12
6½	4	4	3
9½	8	8	8
Total	30	30	23

approximately equal to half the number of twins and of singletons with siblings. This proportion will be found except in the 6½-year group, in which nearly the full quota of only children had been obtained before the change in procedure was decided upon. The distribution of cases is given in Table 1.

The distribution of the 83 sets of twins by like- and unlike-sex pairs at each age level is given in Table 2. The 1:1:1 ratio found in the general population is closely approximated except in the 5½-year group.

In studies of only children there has been little uniformity in defining what constitutes an only child. Some investigators have considered a child "only" if there was more than four years difference between him and the next older or younger sibling; others have made his status at the time of the investigation the only criterion. Thus a child who had lived for the greater part of his life with siblings or in an orphanage or boarding home, but had recently gone to live in a family of adults, would be listed as an only child. For the purposes of this study, which is interested primarily only in the language development of the only child, the following arbitrary rules were adopted:

1. An only child has no living brothers or sisters within nine years of his own age who are members of the same household.

2. A child who had siblings during the age of most rapid acquisition of language, but who had no siblings after the age of four years, is not an only child.

3. A child who has been a permanent resident in a home where other children within nine years of his age were found is not an only child.

Of the 97 only children included in the study, all but three would have qualified for the group under a much more rigid definition. One girl and one boy of 5½ and one boy of 9½ had only grown siblings. There were a few instances of two small families living together because of the depression, but a child coming from a home where this was a permanent arrangement was not classified as an only child. Such questions as the effect of losing a child on the parental relation to the surviving child, or the influence on a child of living alone with two or more generations of adults, are beyond the scope of this study.

Justification for the numerical limits of the only-child group is somewhat difficult. It would have been preferable to make this group proportionate to the distribution of only children in the general population, but we lack accurate figures. Ogburn (97, page 168) states that "the percentage of one-child homes has neither increased nor diminished since 1900, remaining around 25 per cent during the whole period for the sample study of families"; and Wile and Noetzel (151) derive from the 1922 census a distribution in the population of 28.5 per cent only children; but we cannot tell what percentage of these children would satisfy the criterion we have laid down, nor what is the number of only-child homes in various strata of the population. In the Lentz study (72) there were 415 only children in 4,330 cases, or 9.6 per cent. Thirty-four out of 193 or 17.6 per cent of Fenton's (35) kindergarten to sixth-grade subjects were only children, while 73 out of 512 or 14.2 per cent of his university students were only children. Thirteen per cent or 21 out of 162 of Guilford and Worcester's (47) 8A subjects were only children. Nineteen of Terman's thousand gifted children were from one-child families.* In the actual selection of cases it was found that only children are common in the upper social classes, but increasingly rare as we go toward the lower end of the scale. The best solution was to obtain a group of only children representative of the total population, smaller in number than the twins and the singletons with siblings, but large enough to reveal group differences, with the expectation of carrying on a more detailed study of only children at a later date if the findings of this investigation warrant it.

To make the cases representative of the total population of Minneapolis, each group was selected according to the cross-section method of occupational sampling customarily employed at the Institute of Child Welfare of the University of Minnesota. Although most of the data used in the study were collected subsequent to the 1930 census, the new census figures were unfortunately not available in time to base the selection of cases on the latest findings. Between 1920 and 1930 there was a decrease in the percentage of the Minneapolis population whose employment placed them in the three upper occupational groups, and an increase in those falling in the three lower classes. The experimental group therefore has too high a percentage of children drawn from the upper occupational classes to be satisfactorily representative of the 1930 population.

The distribution throughout the occupational categories of twins, singletons with siblings, and only children by age and sex may be found in Appendix II. In general the selection of cases in this regard was fairly accurate.

Deviation in age from proper date for examination. — As is the custom in studies carried on at the Institute of Child Welfare, age groups were chosen so as to be really discrete. The 5½-year group,

---

* Lewis M. Terman *et al.*, *Mental and Physical Traits of a Thousand Gifted Children* (Genetic Studies of Genius, Vol. I, Stanford University Press), p. 115.

for example, was not a group of kindergarten children whose actual ages ranged from 5 to 6 years, with the mean at 5 years and 6 months, but on the date of examination each child was within a few weeks of the exact chronological age at which he was classified. The amount of variation allowed by McCarthy and Day, using groups six months apart in age, was one and one-half months. In the present study the age interval between groups as well as the total length of life for the subjects was greater; hence a deviation of two months for the two younger groups and two and one-half

TABLE 3. — OCCUPATIONAL DISTRIBUTION OF THE EXPERIMENTAL
GROUP AND OF THE MINNEAPOLIS POPULATION

OCCUPATIONAL GROUP*	EXPERIMENTAL GROUP Per Cent	MINNEAPOLIS POPULATION	
		1920† Per Cent	1930‡ Per Cent
I	5.3	5.4	4.2
II	7.6	6.3	9.6
III	32.6	37.3	22.0
All upper groups .	47.7	49.0	35.8
V	26.8	24.3	42.6
VI	15.8	14.9	8.2
VII	9.6	11.8	13.4
All lower groups. .	52.3	51.0	64.2

* Group IV includes only rural population and therefore is not represented in this study.

† Florence L. Goodenough, *The Kuhlman-Binet Tests for Children of Pre-school Age* (Institute of Child Welfare Monograph No. 2, University of Minnesota Press, 1928), pp. 133–36.

‡ Alice M. Leahy, *Measurement of Urban Home Environment* (Institute of Child Welfare Monograph No. 11, University of Minnesota Press, 1936), p. 17.

months for the older group did not seem excessive. Thus the age range of the 5½-year group was from 64 to 68 months; of the 6½-year group, from 76 to 80 months; and of the 9½-year group from 111.5 to 116.5 months. The mean deviation in days from the proper date for examination for each group and subgroup was computed and related to the total chronological age for that group. The same ratio was calculated for McCarthy's subjects, using the group deviations which she gives (Table I, page 26). Although the mean deviation in days is somewhat greater for the subjects of the present study, the total age of her subjects was so much less that the ratios are very similar. It seems probable that the differences in mean age which occur in certain subgroups are negligible for children of the ages under consideration.

Amount of school experience. — In the kindergarten group the amount of school experience previous to examination is a matter of some importance. Since we have no scale which justifies our balancing one week of school experience against one month of chronological age, or any other period, our best procedure is to hold this factor constant. Rigid pairing on this basis was impossible, but the point was kept in mind throughout the investigation. Although no

TABLE 4. — MEAN NUMBER OF WEEKS OF SCHOOL EXPERIENCE IN
THE 5½-YEAR-OLD GROUP

Group	Boys	Girls	Both Sexes
Twins			
Upper occupational	15.3	14.4	14.8
Lower occupational	15.5	12.8	14.2
Both	15.4	13.5	14.5
Singletons			
Upper occupational	17.4	17.3	17.3
Lower occupational	15.4	16.3	15.8
Both	16.3	16.8	16.5
Only children			
Upper occupational	18.4	17.3	17.9
Lower occupational	13.0	18.8	15.7
Both	15.6	18.0	16.8
All			
Upper occupational	16.9	16.2	16.5
Lower occupational	14.9	15.4	15.2
Both	15.8	15.8	15.8

child was interviewed until several weeks after his introduction to the school situation, the complications of irregular attendance or previous nursery school experience were unavoidable. An exact record of the amount of attendance for each child was not obtained, but an approximate figure could be calculated from the known date of enrollment and the date of examination, correcting for prolonged absences due to whooping cough or a broken leg. It was assumed that the effect, if any, of nursery school experience is identical with that of kindergarten experience, and the proper number of weeks was simply added to the records of those subjects who had been in nursery school. The total attendance was expressed in terms of five-day weeks, calculating the figure to the nearest week. The data for all the kindergarten children are given in Table 4. The small group differences found are probably due to chance, but there is a possibility that children from the upper occupational classes enter kindergarten earlier and attend more regularly than children from the lower classes. We may conclude that the 5½-year-old child is likely to have had about two weeks less than a semester of school experience.

All the children except two in the 6½-year group had been in school for a year or longer. A girl from a small town where there

TABLE 5. — GRADE LOCATION OF CHILDREN IN THE 9½-YEAR-OLD GROUP

Group and Grade	Boys	Girls	Both Sexes
Twins			
5B	0	1	1
4A	15	15	30
4B	3	6	9
3A	2	1	3
3B	2	1	3
2A	1	0	1
2B	1	0	1
Percentage at proper grade	62.5	62.5	62.5
Singletons			
4A	23	21	44
4B	3	5	8
Percentage at proper grade	88.5	80.7	84.6
Only children			
4A	5	7	12
4B	5	6	11
3A	2 .	0	2
Percentage at proper grade	41.7	53.8	48.0
All			
5B	0	1	1
4A	43	43	86
4B	11	17	28
3A	4	1	5
3B	2	1	3
2A	1	0	1
2B	1	0	1
Percentage at proper grade	69.3	68.2	68.8

was no kindergarten and a boy whose health had never been good were found in kindergarten. Although the boy cried when asked to come to the examining room, he conversed readily upon arrival, and the girl showed no embarrassment whatever; hence these children were included in their proper age group. All the other 6½-year-old children were in the first half of the first grade.

At 9½ years most children have been in school for four years and a half. Nearly all the subjects included in the 9½-year group had had kindergarten experience, although a few twins attending parochial schools were exceptions. After this length of time it is not likely that a few months more or less would in itself affect the child's adjustment to school or a new situation.

Grade location. — Theoretically, at the age of 9½ years a child who was enrolled in kindergarten at 5 years would be just entering the second half of the fourth grade. The actual range of grade location was from the first half of the second to the first half of the fifth, inclusive. Because of the difficulty in finding cases, it is obvious that the twins would be expected to vary most widely and the only children next, while the singletons would be found in the fourth-grade rooms. As in many other details of sampling, it would have been desirable to control this factor more rigidly, but in practice time and labor had to be conserved. The actual distribution is given in Table 5.

It is possible that the percentage of retardation for twins and only children is higher than for singletons with siblings, but figures obtained from the Board of Education in Minneapolis make it seem probable that the apparent difference is due to the fact that in each school the first room visited was the 4A room. Since 4B pupils were often seated in the same room, it was not necessary to search further to obtain the required number of cases. Twins, however, were located by the fact of twinship, from school records or records of previous studies on file at the Institute of Child Welfare, and were included if of the desired age, sex, and occupational class, irrespective of grade location. Since the location of only children necessitated somewhat persistent search it is not strange that these cases also are spread over a somewhat wide range of grades.

According to the records of the Minneapolis Board of Education for September, 1930, children of 9½ years were to be found in all grades from kindergarten to 6B, inclusive. The percentage in 4A was 30.5; 39.9 per cent were in 4B. These figures are not directly comparable with those in Table 5 because the age group in the whole school population included children whose age was three months above or below the mean, while the variation in the experimental group was not more than two and one-half months; but we are justified in concluding that the experimental group was not below the mean of the Minneapolis school population in grade location.

Selection of subjects in the schools. — Another possible defect in the method of selecting cases lies in the fact that only one or two sets of twins from each school visited were included in the study, while in some of the larger schools fifteen or twenty other children might meet the criteria laid down. We do not know whether being singled out for an interview with a stranger tends to make children embarrassed and self-conscious and thus to inhibit free speech, or whether it gives them self-confidence. It seems probable that young children accompany a stranger to the examining room with less reluctance if they have seen a procession of other children go and return in safety than if the whole experience is novel. It was not feasible to visit every school in the Twin Cities, selecting one or two children from each in order to equalize this factor; but an effort was made to include a few other children from rooms where twins were found, although this could not be done in schools where examining space was at a premium. Often the teacher was consulted in order to avoid selecting a shy child for the first interview. The

TABLE 6. — NUMBER OF SCHOOLS FROM WHICH SUBJECTS WERE
SELECTED AND NUMBER PER SCHOOL

AGE	TWINS		SINGLETONS		ONLY CHILDREN	
	Number of Schools	Subjects per School	Number of Schools	Subjects per School	Number of Schools	Subjects per School
5½	39	2.5	17	5.8	16	3.3
6½	11	2.0	5	4.4	8	2.4
9½	22	2.2	6	8.7	9	2.8

total number of school populations represented in the study and the number of children per school are shown in Table 6. Though the singleton children may be said to have had an advantage in seeing the examiner coming in and out of the school building and the classrooms, the twins always knew that the examiner's interest lay in their twinship, and the only children had the initial advantage of being accustomed to the companionship of adults. Thus the actual advantage or disadvantage of any group is probably negligible.

These possibilities of errors in sampling have probably been discussed in greater detail than is warranted by their actual importance. There is good reason to believe that most children become adjusted to the school situation in a very few days. Almost from the beginning they have contact with a variety of teachers; consequently an experimental situation or a mental test is not radically different from the speech class, the dental examination, or "seeing the nurse," except that it is a little more fun. In most instances discussion with the teacher showed that the child's behavior in the examining room was typical of his schoolroom conduct. Usually the teacher agreed that John talked freely, or that Joseph seldom if ever volunteered a remark, although occasionally a child's uninterested or perverse behavior would be characterized as temperamental. "Patty will either talk your head off, or she won't say anything at all. You never can tell which way she will be." We do not know why one child accompanies his activities with a running fire of verbal comment, while in the same situation his neighbor does not talk at all except in response to definite questions and persistent urging. But certainly it is probable that ease in the examining room and spontaneity of response depend on personality rather than on length of school experience or familiarity with the adult conducting the investigation. Group differences in these phases of behavior will be discussed in a later section. In experimental verification of these ascertained group differences, it would of course be necessary to exercise more rigid control of these sampling errors than was possible in the present investigation.

INTELLIGENCE OF THE SUBJECTS

A single investigator could not administer the Stanford-Binet or any individual test of intelligence to so large a number of subjects, but one of the well-standardized group tests was given in the belief that scores obtained would be valuable in interpreting the data. With the 5½- and 6½-year groups the Pintner-Cunningham Primary Mental Test was used, because Sangren (113) reports that its scores come as close to those of the Binet as any of the tests which he studied. Its intercorrelation with other tests averages higher than any other except the Otis, which has a bad distribution, and its intercorrelation with the Stanford-Binet is higher than that of any other test considered.

In most instances the test was given to several children simultaneously, but never to more than five unless a teacher could be present to assist the children in turning to the right page. Sometimes, because of absence, it was necessary to give the test to one child individually, but there was no indication that the score was affected by this procedure. There was no hard and fast rule as to whether the language record was taken before or after administering the test. In schools where one pair of twins constituted the entire quota of subjects, the simplest procedure was to give the test to both, then retain one twin for the language record, and finally bring back the second twin to obtain his record. Usually when the choice was offered of going back to the classroom alone or remaining to see the toys, the more aggressive twin would volunteer to demonstrate his independence, while the more timid one would remain. If neither proved capable of finding his way about the building alone, the examiner would of course go back with him. It might seem that in this way the twins were given an advantage over the other children in establishing rapport, but on the other hand the experimenter was a complete stranger to the twins more often than to the singletons and only children.

FIG. 1. — MEAN IQ ON PINTNER–CUNNINGHAM TEST FOR CHILDREN FROM THE SIX OCCUPATIONAL GROUPS

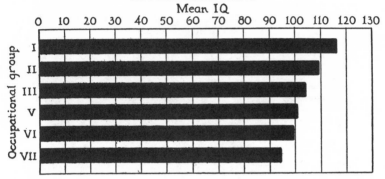

The Pintner-Cunningham Test was given to all of the 248 subjects in the 5½-year group and to all but one of the 63 subjects in the 6½-year group. Figure 1 shows a fairly consistent decrease in mean IQ of these 310 subjects from Group I to Group VII of the occupational scale. This is in keeping with the findings obtained by other investigators using other tests. The difference between the upper and lower classes is statistically reliable, because the ratio of the difference to the standard error of the difference is 4.37. Even for subgroups the difference is always in the same direction, although the amount varies from 2.7 points for only girls to 15.4 points for singleton boys. The mean score for twins is 100.6, for singletons 103.0, and for only children 106.4. The mean for the whole 310 cases is 102.9. For boys the mean is 101.4 and for girls 104.4, but this difference is not statistically reliable. The mean score for twin boys is 98.8, for singleton boys 103.8, and for only boys 101.4. For twin girls the mean score is 102.3, for singleton girls

102.3, and for only girls 111.6. The difference between only girls and twin boys is statistically reliable (critical ratio 3.76), as is that between only girls and all other girls (critical ratio 3.11).

The Pressey Intermediate Classification Test is given to Minneapolis public school pupils soon after they enter the 4A grade. Through the courtesy of the Board of Education, the scores made on this test by 9½-year-old pupils were available. Enough time elapsed between the date of obtaining language records and the compiling of data so that many of the subjects who were retarded had advanced to the grade in which the test is given. The test was given by the examiner to the several sets of 9½-year-old twins from St. Paul or parochial schools. Thus scores were obtained for all but

FIG. 2. — MEAN IQ ON PRESSEY TEST FOR CHILDREN FROM THE SIX
OCCUPATIONAL GROUPS

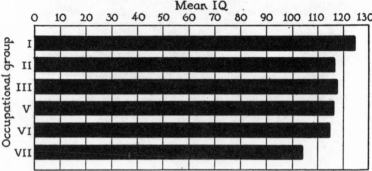

13 of the 125 cases in the 9½-year group. A pair of male twins in Occupational Group VII were of border-line intelligence and too far retarded in school to be given the Pressey Test, but their scores on the Stanford-Binet were available and were assumed to be comparable. The Pressey Test apparently gives an IQ somewhat higher than the Stanford-Binet, but it appears to be satisfactory for differentiating pupils according to relative ability. Figure 2 shows that with the Pressey Test, as with the Pintner-Cunningham Test, there is a progressive although irregular decrease in mean IQ from Group I to Group VII, but the difference between upper and lower socio-economic groups is much less than was noted with the Pintner-Cunningham scores.

As was found on the Pintner-Cunningham Test, the mean score for twins is lower than for singletons and only children. It is markedly low for twin boys from the lower occupational groups. Most investigators (31, 87, 154) have reported lower intelligence test scores for twins than for other children. In the present study the fact that the finding is the same with both the tests used suggests that Stoddard and Wellman (134, pages 125–27) are not justified in their criticism of Day's methodology. Apparently, although the twins were given a preliminary form of the Minnesota Preschool Scale and the Kuhlmann-Binet Test was used with the singletons, the discrepancies in IQ obtained by the two tests were not sufficient to distort or obscure the real difference between the groups. In the present study, of course, the twin-singleton compari-

TABLE 7. — MEAN IQ OF TWINS AND SINGLETONS, AS FOUND BY
DAY (31), McCARTHY (80), AND DAVIS

Investigator	Number of Cases	Test	Mean IQ
		Twins	
Day	123	Minnesota Preschool	94.3
Davis.	118	Pintner-Cunningham	100.6
Davis.	46*	Pressey	111.5
		Singletons	
McCarthy. . . .	133	Kuhlmann-Binet	103.3
Davis.	192	Pintner-Cunningham	104.3
Davis.	66	Pressey	118.3

* The IQ's of two of these subjects were based on Stanford-Binet scores.

sons at each age are based on scores on the same test, the Pintner-Cunningham for the two younger groups and the Pressey Test for the 9½-year group. But in the Pintner-Cunningham Test the child uses no language whatever, while in the Pressey Test reading ability is essential. This finding corroborates Day's conclusion that intelligence test scores are relatively unaffected by the language handicap of twins. When she matched 35 four-year-old twins with single children on the basis of total test scores on the Minnesota Preschool Scale, chronological age, sex, and occupational class, she found that the twins did as well as the singletons on the thirteen verbal items included in the test, although their command of language was much less. In the present study the twins are slightly inferior on both the nonverbal and the verbal scale. Since twins have uniformly been found slightly below other children in intelligence test scores, it is not at all likely that Day's cases were an exception to the general rule.

The Day-McCarthy-Davis data in regard to the intelligence of twins and singletons (including only children) are summarized in Table 7.

CHOICE OF EXPERIMENTAL MATERIAL

To set up a situation capable of holding the interest of both boys and girls ranging in age from 5½ to 9½ years is no simple matter. The existence of a sex difference in play activities and type of toy preferred is an established fact (18, 71, 119), but the degree of prejudice at different ages against entering into activities conceded to be peculiar to the other sex has not been measured. Since no play object or situation was discovered which was of equal appeal to boys and girls of the ages studied, it was decided to choose objects known to be of especial interest to boys. This was done because (1) boys of 5 years are already "conditioned" against girls' toys, but girls if given the opportunity ordinarily enjoy boys' toys; (2) even if they are not interested in the toys, girls can easily be induced to co-operate in the experiment; and (3) since the language development of girls is slightly in advance of that of boys, it is only fair that the advantage, if any, of a high degree of interest in the situation should be given to the boys. If the findings still show superiority on the part of girls, the significance becomes all the greater.

The final selection of a motley collection of little covered wagons with detachable oxen, lassoing cowboys, buffalo hunters, scouts, Indians in attitudes of hostility, flight, or pursuit, and various animals and trees was a happy one. These toys could be easily transported from school to school, were almost certain to stimulate conversation, and lent themselves so readily to manipulation that shyness and self-consciousness were soon forgotten. The younger children tended to set immediately to work standing up and naming the objects, usually exclaiming with delight at their beauty and per-fection of detail. The fourth-grade children were at the age of great delight in Western movies, and were interested in pioneer stories because they were studying early Minnesota history in school. They usually arranged the wagons in a circle, with Indians attacking.

Girls of all ages were likely to examine and identify the objects and then set them up in orderly rows, making a "nice parade," a farm, or a forest. Boys were more inclined to recognize the possi-bilities for action, and immediately set about roping cattle, fighting Indians, and having collisions. Sometimes it appeared that absorp-tion in the toys operated to limit conversation to monosyllables, expletives, and fragmentary remarks, while a child not interested in the toys would converse freely about personal and family affairs, the examiner's belongings, the examining room, or school happenings. At times it seemed that the precariousness with which the horsemen in particular kept their balance tended to limit the amount and quality of conversation. Fisher (36) also found that boys used more fragmentary responses than girls and that boys more often discussed things while girls discussed persons. On the whole it is probable that the type of toy used helped to make the children at ease in the situation and thus predisposed them to spontaneous response.

Although McCarthy and Day used toys and books interchangeably, in this study books were resorted to only when the toys failed of their purpose. The books used for the younger groups were a beautiful collection of ship pictures, a book depicting simple school situations, and a number of gaily colored animal books. For the 9½-year group the ship book was supplemented by a copy of *Slovenly Peter,* which proved unfamiliar and therefore of high interest value in nearly every case.

Ratings were made of the degree of interest shown by each subject in the toys, and in the books when used, according to two simple three-point scales. For the toys these were (1) played with enthusiasm throughout period; (2) showed intermittent interest in toys; and (3) paid little or no attention to toys. For the books they were (1) marked enjoyment of books; (2) moderate degree of interest; and (3) interest slight or none.

Gradations in interest in the experimental material were very clear cut. Some subjects after a few minutes of play would voluntarily begin putting the toys away, or would announce, "I'm through with that book." Others would make no move to engage in play, but would enter into conversation on associated or irrelevant topics. The ratings used, though crude, are not without value. At all ages boys show slightly more interest in the toys than do girls, but there are no age differences. The rating for interest in books has less meaning, for the reason that only about one-fourth of the children were shown the books at all. Occasionally children who were not interested in the toys were enthusiastic over the books, and sometimes a subject who was absorbed in the toys but did not talk while playing would rush pellmell through the books, naming objects as he went, in the hope that he might get at the toys again. Roughly, about twice as many girls as boys were shown the books. In the 5½- and 6½-year groups books were used most often with singleton girls and least often with only girls, but in the 9½-year group no difference was detected. Only boys in the two younger groups were shown the books somewhat oftener than was necessary with twin and singleton boys. In the younger groups books were used in a higher percentage of cases with children from the lower than from the upper occupational classes. Although ratings show a slightly lower degree of interest in books than in toys, this is probably due to the fact that most of the children shown the books were unresponsive because of shyness or lack of rapport.

EXPERIMENTAL SITUATION AND PROCEDURE

All data were obtained in the school buildings and during school hours, thereby saving time and facilitating the work by better control of conditions than is usually possible in the home. An unused room of some sort could always be found, and a low table and chairs installed. Since in the modern school, children are from the beginning accustomed to association with a series of teachers, nurses, and examiners, a statement by the teacher or principal that some of the children were to go with Mrs. Davis to the nurse's room (dining room, library, speech room, or what not) was enough to start the procedure, and thereafter each child, having learned the way, considered it a privilege to escort his successor to the proper place.

Usually rapport was established by a few casual remarks on the way to the examining room or before the toys were produced. If the child did not begin talking freely of his own accord, the examiner framed her remarks in such a way as to stimulate conversation, saying, "I wonder what you play with at home," or "Here are some animals that not many children know," or "Now I'm going to show you something funny." If, after ten minutes with the toys, the child volunteered no remarks, and could not be induced to enter into conversation, the examiner said: "Now we're going to look at some books. I want you to tell me about the pictures."

This procedure may account in part for the fact that the mean length of time needed to obtain fifty responses was somewhat less than in the McCarthy and Day studies. Some such expedient was essential with the occasional child who apparently was accustomed to playing in absolute silence, and certain concessions had to be made to the exigencies of school routine. Young children cannot be detained after the regular time for dismissal because they are expected home on schedule and many mothers cannot be reached by telephone.

With the two younger groups no explanation was given beyond the presentation of the toys and the direction that the child was to play with them. If conversation or questions on the part of the examiner were necessary, the child seemed to get the impression that he was expected to name and discuss the various objects, but spontaneous conversation usually took the same direction. Perhaps because of their longer school experience the 9½-year-olds proved almost certain to play in silence. This group were therefore instructed thus: "I want you to take these toys out of the boxes and play with them any way you like, just as you would if you were at home by yourself. But you must tell me just what you are doing while you play, so I will know."

Wide variation in conversation followed these instructions. Some subjects seemed to feel that they had described the situation adequately in a single sentence, and all the subsequent responses had to be elicited by definite questions. Others burst immediately into a flood of narration which taxed the examiner's powers of recording, and the fifty remarks were obtained without any other stimulation on her part, except perhaps an encouraging nod or smile. Unexpected turns of phrase, descriptive touches, and flights of fancy made the records of the 9½-year-olds an unending source of delight when analysis of the material was undertaken:

His guess was good, for his tomahawk fell and landed on his head.

Now the other men start to charge in, because they knew they were at their doom.

After the cow comes and he sees that they knock him down, he takes a fresh green tree and carries it there to make the prairie look good.

This here old man sees him and tells him he should not shoot his pig, because that's all the pig he's got, and he's had it ten years, and he wants to raise it and make it fat, so if he has a visitor they'll say he's got nice fat pigs.

They're very victorious.

Teachers reported that subjects of this age came back to the classroom beaming and gave such glowing accounts of their experience that those not included in the group were disappointed. "Why is it that some from our room can go downstairs and play cowboy when the rest of us can't?" they would ask. Even at this age, and with the more definite instructions which they were given, the general impression seemed to be that the examiner was interested in what was done rather than in what was said. The writing, they seemed to think, was a description of the situation. Many subjects of their own accord halted in their talk for the writer to catch up. In some instances of torrential talk it was necessary to request the child not to "tell me quite so fast," and occasionally a remark was lost. The procedure in such cases was to omit the remark entirely and go on to the next one. This accounts for some gaps in what would otherwise have been a connected narrative, and possibly tends to lower slightly the total percentage of spontaneous remarks. Sometimes the flood would cease and it would be necessary to interject a question, the answer to which would have to be recorded in place of the omitted spontaneous remark, but such instances were rare, and the writer is convinced that on the whole the records are as exact as though taken in shorthand and transcribed.

Remarks and questions of the examiner were recorded whenever possible. If the subject's conversation was so rapid as to prohibit this, symbols indicated that the remark was elicited or followed a remark of the examiner. The records were made in pencil, with many abbreviations but no words left out. Infantile pronunciations, contractions, and grammatical errors were of course retained. Abbreviations, if not clear, were written out and explanatory notes added after the fifty remarks were obtained and before another subject was brought in. As soon as possible after the record was obtained it was typed, with full explanatory notes to facilitate interpretation. One carbon copy was made, and wide spaces and margins made it possible to use these typed records in the final analyses of the data.

A few practice records showed that the probable extent of vocabulary was not great, and that symbols and abbreviations could be used without the confusion which one would at first suspect. "Indian" was always written "I," "cowboy" as "cb," "covered wagon" as "cw," "black," "brown," or "white horse" by coupling the first two consonants of the adjective with the letter "h." Context showed whether "l.l." meant "looks like" or "little lamb." Only the fact that the range of conversation was so markedly limited by the situation made it possible to make accurate records in longhand of the conversation of children whose mean length of response might reach twelve or fourteen words.

RATING OF THE CHILD'S BEHAVIOR

The child's behavior in the examining room was rated at the close of the interview for shyness, negativism, and distractibility, according to the scale devised by Goodenough and regularly employed by members of the psychometric department at the Institute of Child Welfare. This scale is reproduced in Appendix III. Although the extreme form of each trait was never found, it did not seem worth while to attempt new definitions of terms or finer differentiation, since these records are only incidental to the study. The age of the subjects and their adjustment to school of course account for the fact that only the lesser degrees of the traits were manifested. Even a rating of 3 proved rare.

As we would expect, the only children at all ages are less shy than singletons and twins. Boys are less likely to be shy than girls, and at 9½ less shyness was noted than in the younger groups. Very little negativism was found, and there were no differences with age, but boys were slightly less negativistic than girls. Girls were somewhat more distractible than boys, perhaps because they were less interested in the situation, and distractibility was found to decrease with age.

In addition to Goodenough's scale, a seven-step scale for talkativeness was devised:

1. Child exceedingly voluble throughout interview; no remarks elicited.
2. Child converses readily and regularly; few remarks elicited.
3. Child shows initial shyness, but remarks are mainly voluntary.
4. Remarks slow, but fairly regular; no definite attempt at eliciting necessary.
5. Response slow, obtained mainly by use of questions.
6. Very little spontaneous speech, although "set" for naming pictured objects may be built up.
7. All responses elicited.

These ratings revealed a consistent tendency toward greater talkativeness in boys than in girls, and in children in the upper occupational group as compared with children in the lower occupational group. At 5½ and 6½ years only girls were most talkative of all subgroups, but this was not true at 9½. The difference between upper and lower occupational groups had largely disappeared in the 9½-year group, probably because of school experience.

Goodenough and her associates (43) concluded that nursery school experience tended somewhat to increase talkativeness in preschool children. In the 5½-year group the coefficient of correlation

(Pearson product-moment method) between talkativeness and length of school experience was .02.

LENGTH OF TIME REQUIRED TO OBTAIN FIFTY REMARKS

Time was taken to the nearest minute by an ordinary watch at the beginning and end of the observation period. The range was from five to forty-five minutes, but some group differences appear. The mean time was least for the 5½-year group and greatest for the 6½-year group. The difference between the 5½-year group and the other age groups is statistically reliable. The mean time is slightly

TABLE 8. — MEAN NUMBER OF MINUTES REQUIRED TO OBTAIN FIFTY
REMARKS AND CRITICAL RATIOS BETWEEN GROUPS

MEASURE	AGE GROUP			ALL TWINS ($N=166$)	ALL SINGLETONS ($N=173$)	ALL ONLY CHILDREN ($N=97$)
	5½ Years ($N=248$)	6½ Years ($N=63$)	9½ Years ($N=125$)			
Mean. . .	12.75	15.79	15.09	13.66	14.47	13.07
SD. . . .	6.44	6.28	5.54	6.88	5.52	6.10
σ_m	0.41	0.79	0.49	0.53	0.42	0.62

Critical Ratios between Groups
5½ and 6½ . . 3.39   Twins and singletons 2.68
5½ and 9½ . . 3.59   Singletons and only children . . 3.07
Upper- and lower-class girls 2.49
Upper- and lower-class children . . 1.78

greater for girls than for boys, and for children in the lower occupational groups. The difference between upper- and lower-class boys is slight, but between upper- and lower-class girls it is more than two minutes. These differences are consistently in the same direction, although not of sufficient magnitude to satisfy the criterion for statistical reliability. The mean time is least for the only children and greatest for the singletons. The pattern is much the same for the subgroups at all ages, except that the 6½-year-old twins exceed the singletons and the 9½-year-old only children exceed the twins. Time increases with age for singletons and only children, but in twins the time is five minutes longer at the 6½-year level than at the 9½-year level. This is probably an error of sampling. Critical ratios are given in Table 8.

The length of the observation period in McCarthy's study ranged from seven to fifty minutes with the mean at 19.3; Day's mean time was 14.9 minutes. In the present study the mean for all ages was 13.6. Coefficients of correlation at each age indicate a slight negative relationship between length of time and intelligence; that is, the brighter children tend to make their remarks in a shorter time. In McCarthy's (79) study of children's language in different situations the correlation between the number of times a child was found talking and the time score was —.50.

III. ARTICULATION

Previous Investigations of Articulation

The amateur biographers to whom we are so greatly indebted for our knowledge of most phases of language development have largely ignored the course of progress in articulation. Preyer (105) drew a parallel between disturbances of speech in adults and imperfections in the speech of the child, and made minute observations of his son's progress toward perfect articulation during the first three years. Stevenson (132) noted analogies between the mispronunciations of children and the speech of foreigners, and believed that these imperfections could be classified according to Grimm's law. Tracy (144), the first to attempt really quantitative work, analyzed twelve vocabularies of children from 19 to 30 months old recorded by persons in whose accuracy he had confidence. He tabulated his findings first by the initial sound of the word and then by types of faulty production of sounds, giving the relative frequency of misuse in the initial, medial, and final position. The most difficult sounds, he concludes, are *r*, *l*, and *th*, and the easiest *m*, *p*, and *b*. He notes the frequent mispronunciation of double consonants and suggests that the choice of a substitute sound is often determined by the occurrence of an easier sound in the syllable immediately preceding or following, causing the easy sound to be reduplicated and the difficult one not attempted. Stern (131) distinguishes sensorial, apperceptive, and motor mistakes, and mistakes of reproduction. Motor mistakes he considers due to imperfect development of the speech organs. He also believes that the child's mutilations of words follow the laws of word change which have been established in the history of speech. Major (82) traced a child's pronunciation of 62 words from the thirteenth to the thirty-sixth month.

McCarthy (80) reported no findings as to articulation or pronunciation in the 140 preschool children whose language development she studied, although she was careful to record the responses exactly as they sounded. Great improvement in articulation with age is shown by the increase in the percentage of responses that were comprehensible to her. At 18 months 74 per cent of all responses were incomprehensible, at 24 months 33 per cent, and at 30 months 11 per cent.

Day's (31) percentage of incomprehensible responses at 2 years was less than McCarthy's, probably because of her greater familiarity with young children, but at 3 and 4 years the twins are somewhat less readily understood than the singletons, a fact that is of interest in view of the findings regarding articulation of twins given in the present study. Day rated articulation as clear, average, or poor, a classification that is rough but nevertheless differentiates well enough to show improvement with age and slight superiority in girls and in children from the upper socio-economic classes.

Wellman and her associates (149) studied the speech sounds of 204 children from 2 to 6 years old. They found that at 5 years from 87 to 90 per cent of the various speech elements were given correctly. Girls tended to be superior to boys on the consonants.

The value of speech correction during the preschool years has been demonstrated by Sommers (127) and Springob (128), using experimental and control pairs. Improvement after a twelve-week interval was noted in both groups, but the gain was twice as great for the experimental group.

With a view to determining the extent of personality, intellectual, and language handicaps, Remer (107) studied 734 children just entering school. The list of possible handicaps was prepared in advance, with careful definition of each trait, and teachers used these while collecting data, scoring handicaps as mild, moderate, and serious. The writer talked with the teacher and observed the children both during and after school. The obtained figures list "baby talk" or stuttering and stammering in only 3 per cent of the cases, but such tendencies as "meager vocabulary" or "speech not clear" bring the total of language-handicapped children to about 10 per cent of all those studied.

Greater difficulty with articulation on the part of boys has been universally reported. Jespersen (60, page 146) suggests that the pronunciation of the little girls is "not spoilt by the many bad habits and awkwardnesses so often found in boys." Girls may "get into other people's way of talking" easier than boys because of their liking for the conventional, whereas boys are often reluctant to do as others do. He believes that there is greater originality in the language of boys, since they are more interested in words as such and in the acoustics of language. Sommers (127) reports fewer defects and greater improvement in girls. Every survey of speech defects mentions the enormous sex difference, particularly in stuttering.

Morrison (89) studied speech defects of 218 children in four kindergarten and four first-grade classes. No child was under 5 years old, and only eight were over 7, the majority being a little over 6. She found that 49 per cent did not give *th* correctly (one-third of the 49 per cent came from foreign-language homes, where this sound is not used), but only 12.8 per cent showed other marked errors in articulation. Defects were accompanied by enlarged adenoids, tonsils, and glands. She thinks it probable that incorrect habits persisting at 5 and 6 years may remain uncorrected if the child is given no assistance.

Town (142) grouped her forty-two 5- and 6-year-old children as (1) those having no speech difficulty that could not be eradicated by regular classroom training, and (2) those requiring special training. She found one child who was understood only by his younger brother of 5, "who not only understands him, but talks in the same way while conversing with him though using normal articulation when talking to other people." Stinchfield (133) decided on each of three occasions when pairs of twins possessing "twin language" were brought to her clinic that the condition was in reality only persistence of infantile pronunciations.

Lima (75) found letter substitutions occurring mainly in the first and second grades. Seventy-five per cent of the 6- and 7-year-olds who were being treated for speech defects were in this group.

Carrell (21) reports that of 1,174 children at Mooseheart over 5 years old, 10 per cent were speech defectives. Ages are not given, but the Kuhlmann-Anderson intelligence score and the Stanford Achievement are consistently lower for the defective group than for the general Mooseheart population, the relation varying directly with severity of defect. Furthermore, slightly more than 28 per cent of speech defectives had hearing losses as measured by the Western Electric 4-A Audiometer, while only 9 per cent of the control group had similar losses in auditory acuity.

The relationship between speech defect and intelligence has been known since the beginning of the school surveys. Wallin (148) found that about one-fourth of the children in the special classes in St. Louis had defective speech. Town (143), studying the language development of 285 idiots and imbeciles, found stammering in the speech of 60 per cent of the low-grade and 43 per cent of the high-grade imbeciles. Root (109) found that pupils afflicted with indistinct speech were least able to make normal school progress. Conradi (26) found the average age at each grade higher for the stutterer, not because of mental inferiority but because of neglect and sensitiveness. Murray (90), using silent reading tests, found stutterers one grade below normal in comprehension and two grades below in rate. When intelligence was considered, the disparity was increased a half grade further. As a rule stutterers, unlike other speech defectives, have not been found below normal in intelligence. The recent work of Meltzer (86) and Hawthorne (49) indicates greater talkativeness in stuttering children. Payne (100) believes that mispronunciation of words due to novelty, length, or poor example is often wrongly considered pathological.

The whole question of speech defect is complicated by variations in terminology and definition, but investigators agree that while stuttering increases in prevalence throughout the school grades, the percentage of other defects decreases very decidedly.

METHOD OF MEASURING ARTICULATION

One reason for the decision to concentrate this investigation at the kindergarten level was the discovery made during the preliminary stages that there are great differences in perfection of articulation among kindergarten children. This necessitated a careful analysis of the data on the basis of articulation, since group differences detected in this phase of speech development might be highly significant. The undertaking was complicated by the fact that the examiner had had no formal training in the detection or classification of speech defects and consequently could undertake only the most elementary analysis. For this analysis a seven-step scale was devised:

1. Articulation perfect.*
2. Tendency to mumble or slur all speech, or occasional difficulty with one specific sound.
3. Consistent difficulty with one sound, or occasional difficulty with more than one sound.
4. Consistent difficulty with more than one sound, but articulation otherwise clear enough for ready comprehension.
5. Consistent difficulty with several sounds; articulation in general rather good.
6. Speech not readily understood.
7. Speech almost incomprehensible.

In applying this scale, enunciation was rated as perfect unless

* Stuttering was disregarded, but all records were reclassified on the basis of stuttering.

the record showed more than two lapses, on the ground that the experimenter might have misunderstood the child's production of the sound in question, and conversely might have missed an occasional lapse on the part of another child. Obviously, when a single worker had to stimulate the child's speech, answer his questions, and make a phonetic record of what he said, occasional mistakes were bound to occur. The results of this analysis are presented with considerable hesitation, in the belief that they warrant a repetition of the work by a better-qualified investigator. Two recorders would be desirable, one to make sure of the subject matter, the other to note articulation.

Although the speech correction program is well developed in Minneapolis and St. Paul schools, and although the Board of Education and the Speech Correction Department gave excellent cooperation both by allowing the investigator access to records and by making it possible for her to discuss individual cases with teachers, a quantitative analysis of the language records was nevertheless necessary in order to obtain a reliable picture of the distribution of speech defects among the kindergarten population. In spite of the policy of the department that speech correction be given as early as possible, lack of funds and crowded buildings limit the holding of speech classes in most districts to alternate years. Since kindergarten children attend school only a half day, it is sometimes impossible to arrange for the presence of all children needing the service. In some of the poorer sections of the city, where foreign languages are prevalent and the cultural level of the home is low, a minor defect such as difficulty with *th* or *r* will be the rule rather than the exception, while in another type of community the same defect would immediately place the child in a correction class. Finally, in some instances the findings of the speech correction teacher are not corroborated by the performance of the child in a play situation. A child may be able to produce a sound correctly in the examining room even though he habitually misses it; conversely, a child in the test situation may have difficulty with a sound which ordinarily he manages correctly.

RESULTS OBTAINED BY ARTICULATION SCALE

Five-and-a-half-year group. — Consistent difficulty with specific sounds is comparatively rare. Most kindergarten children are able to produce all sounds correctly at least part of the time. This finding is in keeping with those obtained by students of child development in other traits. It is probable that elimination of speech infantilisms proceeds with occasional lapses but that gradual improvement takes place from week to week or month to month, just as has been found in walking, acquisition of bladder control, and outgrowing the day-time nap. Pillsbury and Meader (103, page 218) give definite evidence that even a highly educated adult varies widely in the movements with which he repeatedly pronounces the same word.

The percentage of kindergarten children in the several subgroups who had perfect articulation is given in Table 9. The percentage is considerably higher for girls than for boys, both in the upper and

TABLE 9. — PERCENTAGE OF 5½-YEAR-OLD GROUP HAVING PERFECT ARTICULATION

Group	Boys	Girls	Both Sexes
Twins			
Upper occupational	48.6	65.2	56.8
Lower occupational	22.2	52.0	36.5
Both	33.3	58.3	45.8
Singletons			
Upper occupational	62.5	91.3	76.6
Lower occupational	76.0	74.1	75.0
Both	69.4	82.0	75.7
Only children			
Upper occupational	92.3	92.3	92.3
Lower occupational	57.1	76.9	66.7
Both	74.1	84.6	79.2
All			
Upper occupational	63.8	81.3	72.6
Lower occupational	50.0	66.1	58.0
Both	56.4	73.4	64.9

in the lower occupational groups, and markedly lower for twins than for singletons and only children. In Figure 3 the performance of the singletons at each age is taken as 100 per cent, and the twins are compared with the singletons on this basis. At 5½ years the articulation of twins is 60 per cent that of singletons; at 6½, 90 per cent; and at 9½, 97 per cent. Since McCarthy did not measure articulation at all, and Day used only a rough rating of clear, fair, and poor, we have no means of comparing these findings with those of the earlier studies. Analyses made in the present study and reported on pages 38–41 show that children with faulty articulation are inferior to those with no defects in many phases of language development. It is highly probable that an enormous difference in

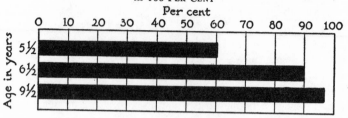

FIG. 3. — PERCENTAGE OF TWINS HAVING PERFECT ARTICULATION AT SUCCESSIVE AGE LEVELS WHEN SINGLETONS ARE TAKEN AS 100 PER CENT

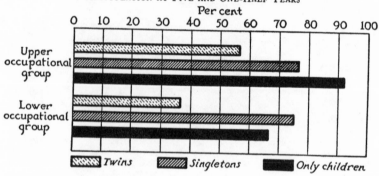

FIG. 4.—PERCENTAGE OF TWINS, SINGLETONS, AND ONLY CHILDREN FROM UPPER AND LOWER OCCUPATIONAL GROUPS HAVING PERFECT ARTICULATION AT FIVE AND ONE-HALF YEARS

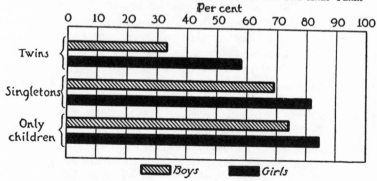

FIG. 5.—SEX DIFFERENCES IN PERCENTAGE OF TWINS, SINGLETONS, AND ONLY CHILDREN HAVING PERFECT ARTICULATION AT FIVE AND ONE-HALF YEARS

34

the articulation of preschool twins and singletons passed unnoticed because both groups of children were not handled by a single investigator.

Contrary to the findings in other phases of the study, the only children were not greatly superior to the singletons in articulation. There was a difference between singleton and only boys of the upper occupational group, but in the lower group the difference was in favor of the singletons. A comparison of upper and lower occupational groups is shown in Figure 4.

Six-and-a-half-year group. — The improvement in articulation for the first-grade children is great enough to indicate that the critical period is past. Perfect articulation was found for 81.8 per cent of twins, 90.9 per cent of singletons, and 89.5 per cent of only children. Of the boys, 81.2 per cent, and of the girls, 93.5 per cent received the perfect score. No child received a score higher than 3 on the articulation scale, but, since there were only 63 children in the entire 6½-year group, this is probably due to sampling rather than to scarcity of severe defects at this age. In one school twin boys, both of whom had perfect articulation, were selected as the quota for Occupational Group VI. Had the examiner chanced to postpone her visit to that school until two months later, these boys would have been beyond the age limits set up, and a set would have been chosen who suffered from a speech defect so severe as to make them as nearly incomprehensible as any child encountered at the kindergarten age.

Nine-and-a-half-year group. — At 9½ only vestiges of articulatory difficulty remain. Perfect articulation was scored for 87.5 per cent of twins, 90.4 per cent of singletons, and 100 per cent of only children. The score was perfect for 87.1 per cent of boys and 95.2 per cent of girls. The difficulties which persist are very slight, with no score given beyond 2. Several of the children had had speech correction, and one or two twins were still receiving it.

Difficulty with Specific Sounds

Five-and-a-half-year group. — The digraph *th*, especially in the initial position, is by all odds the greatest stumbling block. The most common substitution is *d* for *th*, which occurs 643 times, 429 times on boys' records and 214 times on those of girls. There were 45 instances of substituting *f*, *s*, or *z* for *th*, and initial *th* was elided on 21 occasions. " 'Em" for "them," which is universal in the rapid speech even of adults, was not included in this list. The next most frequent substitution was *w* for *r*, which occurred 81 times in boys and 32 times in girls. Third in frequency of occurrence is the substitution of *t* or *th* for *s* — the substitution popularly known as the lisp. The findings lend support to the universal belief that it is a feminine peculiarity, for it was noted only three times in boys but 78 times in girls. Initial *s* was elided 51 times. Substitution of *d* for *g* and of *t* for hard *c* occurred 44 times each. There were only two vowel substitutions. Many other substitutions were noted, but their occurrence was infrequent.

The total number of lapses noted was 811 for twins, 215 for singletons, and 163 for only children. Of the 1,189 instances, 678 were found on the records of boys and 511 on those of girls. Forty different defects and substitutions were noted. Thirty-six of these were found on the records of twins and 17 on those of singletons, but only 10 on those of only children. This fact is interesting when we note that the total number of lapses per child is a little higher for only children than for singletons. It appears that the only child has fewer defects, but is more consistent in his faulty articulation than is the singleton with siblings. Also, more different defects were noted in girls than in boys — 33 as against 23 — although the total number of lapses was considerably less for girls than for boys.

Six-and-a-half-year group. — Substitution of *d* for *th* was noted on nine first-grade records, with a total of 154 instances. Initial *th* was dropped in two instances, occurring on two different records, and *f* was substituted for *th* in one instance. Substitution of *d* for *j* occurred twice on one record. Of the total 159 lapses, 96 occurred in twins, 50 in singletons, and 13 in only children. Thirty examples were found on the records of girls and 129 on the records of boys.

Nine-and-a-half-year group. — The only sound with which children of this age have difficulty is the digraph *th*. One or more instances of substituting *d* for *th* were found on the records of nine boys, the total number of instances being 40. There was also one instance of "t'row" for "throw." The three girls who received a rating of 2 on the articulation scale had no difficulty with any specific sound, but their trouble was slurring and poor enunciation. One twin girl, whose mean length of sentence nevertheless was 11.96 words, had been receiving treatment for years for "lateral lisp," and her sister, although she had never been listed as a speech defective, impressed the examiner as having sufficiently poor enunciation to warrant a rating of 2. Her teacher concurred in this judgment.

BILINGUALISM

The precise relationship between faulty articulation and bilingualism in the home cannot be determined from the data obtained in this study. Whenever a home visit was made, or when the teacher could supply the information, a note was made in regard to the use of a foreign language. One set of first-grade twin boys from a German-speaking home substituted *d* for *th* 71 times. It might be argued that this was due to the fact that *th* in English is regularly *d* in German, but the same phenomenon was noted in children of pure English descent. Although, as Morrison (91) has pointed out, the *th* sound is lacking in many foreign languages, this fact does not account for the well-nigh universal substitution of *d*. The occurrence of "t'ing," "t'row," and "t'rough" is extremely rare in comparison with "dis," "dat," "dese," and "dose." On the other hand, not a single instance was noted of the substitution of *v* for *w* or of *y* for *j*, both of which are notoriously common in the Scandinavian immigrant, and flawless articulation was sometimes found even at 5½ years in children whose parents spoke no English whatever. Pending further investigation we cannot conclude that for children who have the example of perfect production of English sounds by older children or adults outside the home, the faulty articulation of foreign-born parents is a major handicap.

STUTTERING

In the consideration of articulatory defects according to the articulation scale the occurrence of stuttering was disregarded, but stuttering was noted in six twin boys and one singleton boy in the 5½-year group and in one twin boy in the first-grade group. Reference to the records of the speech department showed that several children in the 9½-year group had stuttered at some time during their school experience, but the records of the experimental study revealed no trace of this difficulty. Three of the stuttering boys had an articulation rating of 1, two a rating of 3, two of 4, and the remaining one was given a rating of 5. This suggests that stuttering in children six years old or less may accompany poor articulation, and that difficulty in making oneself understood may be a causative factor in stuttering. In no case was the degree of stuttering at all severe.

DISCUSSION OF FINDINGS

We should expect these findings concerning perfection of articulation to be reflected in the child's personality and behavior and in other phases of language development. At this point, therefore, let us compare the child whose articulation is faulty with the child whose articulation is perfect.

Quantitative evidence of differences in personality and behavior between children in the 5½-year group having perfect articulation and those having speech defects was obtained by comparing the ratings of the two sets of children on the various scales which were employed. Of the 248 children making up the 5½-year group 160 had perfect articulation and 88 had a greater or less degree of speech defect. On the talkativeness scale 103 or 64.4 per cent of the children with perfect articulation received ratings of 1 or 2, while 42

TABLE 10. — PERCENTAGE OF PERFECT AND DEFECTIVE SPEAKERS
IN THE 5½-YEAR GROUP GIVEN A RATING OF 1 ON
BEHAVIOR TRAITS *

Behavior Trait	Percentage of Perfect Speakers	Percentage of Defective Speakers
Talkativeness (1 or 2) . . .	64.4	47.7
Shyness	75.0	71.6
Negativism.	95.6	90.9
Distractibility	87.5	96.6
Interest in situation	72.5	77.3

* For a description of the behavior scales see pages 21 and 25 and Appendix III.

or 47.7 per cent of the children with defective articulation received these ratings. Comparing the ratings for interest in the situation, on the other hand, 116 or 72.5 per cent of the perfect speakers were given a rating of 1, but 68 or 77.3 per cent of the defective speakers received this rating. There is a suggestion that the defective speakers are somewhat less distractible and slightly more shy and negativistic than the perfect speakers. Very little value can be attached to these ratings, however, because they were given by the examiner herself on the basis of her single interview with the subject. The findings according to the rating scales are summarized in Table 10.

More objective evidence of the connection between good articulation and command of language may be obtained from the language records. The mean length of response for the 160 children with perfect articulation was 4.85 words, but for the 88 with some degree of speech defect it was 4.00. This difference is statistically reliable, a rather striking finding in view of the fact that many of the speech defects listed were so slight that the child's conversation was readily comprehensible, even to a stranger. The mean time required to obtain fifty remarks was slightly more for the defective group, but this difference was not statistically reliable. The coefficient of correlation (Pearsonian r) between length of remark and length of time at $5\frac{1}{2}$ years was $-.31\pm.03$ for the children with perfect articulation and $-.14\pm.07$ for those with defective articulation.

Children with perfect articulation tended toward greater spontaneity of speech than did those who still experienced difficulty in producing one or more of the speech sounds. Since this difference was particularly noticeable in girls it may mean that a sex difference which will be discussed in a later section is intensified by poor articulation. In the case of twin boys, so many of whom betrayed difficulties with articulation, the mean number of spontaneous remarks for those with speech defects was greater than for those without. These boys, of course, are accustomed to conversing with each other in spite of poor articulation. Also, there may be a sampling error, since 34 of these boys have speech defects, and only 14 do not. Again in the case of only girls the findings are the reverse of the general trend, but there are only four girls in this group with defective articulation and 22 with perfect articulation. The findings indicate that girls who have articulatory difficulty are more reluctant to talk, at least in the presence of a stranger, than are boys with the same difficulty. The difference between twin girls with and twin girls without a defect is statistically reliable, but for the group as a whole it is not (critical ratios 3.01 and 2.24, respectively).

Marston (85) considered the number of questions asked a rough measure of extroversion. Since asking questions is voluntary, we should expect that children who were reluctant to talk would refrain from this type of conversation. The records show that a small but consistent difference does exist. Children with perfect articulation asked an average of 6.2 questions, while the mean for those with speech defects was 5.4; but the difference is not statistically reliable.

When the speech difficulty is severe the child's responses tend to be limited to names of objects, usually elicited only after some urging. An extreme example of this is the twin girl Mattie, one of many children from the home of a foreign-born laborer. Other children in the family had been slow, but the kindergarten teacher found the twins unique, in her long experience, in their negativism and inability to use language. The twin sister Millie could with urging pronounce isolated words such as "man," "dog," "boy," "pig," and "sheep," but her attempts at combining words were barely comprehensible. Twelve minutes were spent in eliciting 86 words. Mattie's behavior in the examining room is described by the note written at the time: "Mattie's language ability is practically nonexistent. She can produce a few sounds, but does not do so voluntarily. During the first ten minutes of observation she played busily, but did not utter a sound nor answer a question. The toys were finally taken away, books substituted, and she was told that she could not play with the toys any more until she told what the pictures were about." Twenty-eight minutes of this drastic treatment elicited 20 different enunciations which might be leniently called words. The total of 51 utterances consisted for the most part of "titty," "dook," "doggie," and "hortie," but there were also attempts to pronounce names of other common objects, such as "o'nge" (orange) and "shickie."

Obviously when a child thus handicapped attempts to construct a sentence we encounter a persistence at the kindergarten age of the infantile structure ordinarily outgrown at three years. Nonessential words are omitted or slurred, and the child's efforts are directed toward making his hearer understand his central meaning, without regard to the finer shades. We find such sentences as "He t'ootin' tow," "She p'ayin' wiv tats," "Dot one bwoken arm," "Dere two guys widing" in the records of children who made exceptionally high scores on the Pintner-Cunningham Test.

One bright girl by confining her responses to single words which she had mastered prevented the examiner from detecting her speech difficulty at all. She pointed out objects in books, naming them readily and using a total of 74 words. Subsequently she made a score on the Pintner-Cunningham Test which gave her an IQ of 128. It was while discussing this finding with the teacher that the fact of her difficulty with articulation came to light. Since the actual record showed no defect, this child was not classed as having a speech difficulty, and it is very possible that in other cases taciturnity was due to articulation rather than shyness.

The differences in language ability between the 5½-year-old children with perfect articulation and those with defective speech are summarized in Table 11. Although not all the differences are statistically reliable, the evidence is so consistent as to make it extremely probable that faulty articulation tends to retard general language development through the kindergarten year.

The shorter sentence length found among those in the 5½-year

TABLE II. — COMPARATIVE LANGUAGE ABILITY OF 5½-YEAR-OLD CHILDREN HAVING PERFECT AND FAULTY ARTICULATION

MEASURE	GROUP WITH PERFECT ARTICULATION ($N=160$)			GROUP WITH FAULTY ARTICULATION ($N=88$)			CRITICAL RATIO
	Mean	SD	σ_m	Mean	SD	σ_m	
Words per sentence. . .	4.85	1.30	....	4.00	1.45	....	4.39
Number of minutes. . .	12.87	3.18	.25	13.77	3.26	.35	2.09
Number of different words.	102.2	22.65	1.79	82.5	26.05	2.78	5.95
Number of subordinate clauses	6.7	.....	....	4.3	.....	....	....
Number of questions . .	6.2	.....	....	5.4	.....	....	...
Number of spontaneous remarks							
Boys	41.2	12.4	1.51	39.1	15.6	2.07	1.08
Girls	40.2	13.4	1.4	31.3	19.8	3.45	2.39

group having speech difficulty does not hold for the older children, but this is not strange in view of the small number of cases and the very minor nature of the defects which persist. The mean sentence length for the eight in the 6½-year group who have a defect is 5.40; for the 55 others, 5.26 words. In the 9½-year group the mean length for the eleven children having defects is 6.69 and for the 114 others, 6.53 words.

It is probable that in this difficulty with articulation, often persisting in twins until about the age of 6 years, but usually disappearing in singletons well before the age of entering kindergarten, lies the explanation of the marked language retardation found by Day in her preschool twins as compared with the singleton children studied by McCarthy. This faulty articulation would account for the greater number of incomprehensible responses in the twins at 3 and 4 years. It would explain the shorter sentences, the higher percentage of naming and of emotionally toned remarks, and the lower percentage of questions. It would account for the markedly greater number of remarks which are functionally complete but structurally incomplete, and for the lesser use of verbs, adjectives, pronouns, conjunctions, and prepositions. Furthermore, it affords a reasonable explanation for the increasing superiority of the singletons during the period from 36 to 54 months. It is precisely during this time that the singletons are rapidly eliminating their faulty articulation and are making a phenomenal advance in sentence structure. The twins, on the other hand, are still struggling to make their infantile pronunciations understood and are consequently limited to the essential words which form the skeleton of a sentence.

The variability in articulation found in twins during the kindergarten year is just what we should expect during the period when they succeed in discarding their language handicap. Some already have perfect articulation, others are conversing fluently in spite of a remnant of infantilism, while a third group are making little progress. In mean length of sentence they are abreast of the ordinary singleton with siblings, but have not equaled the performance of the only child. In the functional use of language only negligible differences remain.

Summary

1. A seven-step scale was devised as a crude method of expressing the degree of perfection of articulation.

2. At $5\frac{1}{2}$ years all degrees of articulation are encountered, from perfection down to practical incomprehensibility. No severe defects were found in the older groups.

3. The articulation of girls is superior to that of boys, and that of children from the upper occupational groups to that of children from the lower occupational groups.

4. The articulation of twins at $5\frac{1}{2}$ years is markedly inferior to. that of other children.

5. Children with faulty articulation tend to use short sentences and a limited vocabulary and to lack spontaneity of response.

6. The digraph *th* proved the most difficult sound at all ages.

IV. LENGTH OF SENTENCE

Previous Investigations

Since Nice (94) in 1925 called attention to the value of the mean length of remark as a measure of linguistic development in children, a number of investigators, notably Smith (122), McCarthy (80), and Day (31), have verified and added to her conclusions. Smith found a steady increase in mean length of remark up to the age of 4½ years, but the amount of gain lessened after the age of 3½, while there was very great variability in the older children, although they showed the same mental ability. For this reason she questioned the value of the measure for children over 4 years of age. McCarthy found that children of the three upper socio-economic classes used longer sentences than those belonging to the three lower classes. The difference is statistically reliable in the 3- and 4-year-old children. She also pointed out a tendency for those children associating mainly with adults to use longer sentences than those who spent most of their time with children. The mean length of remark for Day's 5-year-old twins was slightly below that of the 3-year-old singletons, and critical ratios ($D/\sigma_{diff.}$) were of high reliability at 2, 3, and 4 years. Howard's (55) sets of preschool triplets also were greatly retarded in sentence length as compared with McCarthy's singletons. The mean length for her 5-year-old triplets was 2.98 words. Stalnaker (129) reports a mean length of 4.67 words for fourteen preschool children from the upper socio-economic classes ranging in age from 2:4 to 4:0 years. This is approximately the same finding as that obtained by McCarthy for comparable groups. In written language, LaBrant (69) found among her group of school children that girls used more words per theme, but not more words per clause. Her adult subjects, however, used 15.2 words per clause, while the fourth- to eighth-grade pupils used 7.2 words per clause. Stormzand's (135) average sentence length for fourth-grade compositions was 11.1 words, with a progressive increase each year to 21.5 words for university upper classmen. Davis (30) found a statistically reliable difference in length of questions asked by younger and older children, and the mean length of questions was greater for girls than for boys.

Rules for Counting Words and Dividing Sentences

Word count. — In general the rules for counting words were those laid down by McCarthy and followed by Day, but in doubtful cases a note was made of the decision so that the procedure might be uniform throughout the study. The intention was to count as one word those expressions which probably function as a unit in the child's understanding, but there are instances where it would be hard to find logical justification for the decision.

"Oh boy," "my gosh," "darn it," "doggone it" scored as one word.
"All right," "maybe," "giddy-up," "someone" scored as one word.
"Lighthouse," "birdhouse," "high school" scored as one word.
"Oh yes," "oh no," "oh gee" as two words.
"Let's see" as two words.
"On to" as two words.
"Christmas tree" as two words.
"Kinda," "oughta," "hafta" as two words.

Sentence division. — The following rules were followed in determining sentence division:

1. The remark was considered finished if the child came to a complete stop, either letting the voice fall, giving interrogatory or exclamatory inflection, or indicating clearly that he did not intend to complete the sentence.

2. When one simple sentence was immediately followed by another with no pause for breath, they were considered one sentence if the second statement was clearly subsidiary to the first. Woodcock (160) points out that ideas of "why," "because," and "if" are first expressed in just this way, and unless they are written as one sentence the meaning is lost. This was LaBrant's (69) reason for making the clause rather than the sentence the unit of measurement. Examples are: "I have a sister, she's in the fourth grade"; "There was buffaloes, no there wasn't buffaloes, there was maneaters"; "I used to have, my brother used to have, a tricycle."

Findings

DIFFERENCES IN SENTENCE LENGTH IN DIFFERENT AGE, SEX, AND OCCUPATIONAL GROUPS

Table 12 shows the mean sentence length for children from each of the six occupational classes at each age level. As McCarthy (80) found with preschool children, the trend is definitely downward from Group I to Group VII. The mean length for Group VII in the 9½-year group is less than that for Group I in the 5½-year group. At the kindergarten age it seems clear that children from Group I maintain the distinct linguistic superiority over all other occupational groups which McCarthy discovered in younger children. The large number of cases in the 5½-year group makes it

TABLE 12. — MEAN NUMBER OF WORDS PER REMARK MADE BY CHILDREN IN SIX OCCUPATIONAL GROUPS

Age in Years	Occupational Group					
	I	II	III	V	VI	VII
5½	5.68	4.91	4.64	4.54	4.37	3.69
6½	4.90	6.01	5.61	5.52	4.48	4.57
9½	6.51	6.80	6.93	6.78	6.00	5.37
All	5.73	5.70	5.44	5.28	4.83	4.40

probable that the findings accurately picture the true state of affairs, but in the 6½- and 9½-year groups, Group I includes so few cases that sampling may account for the apparent loss of this advantage by children from the professional class. For the number of cases in each group at each age, the reader is referred to Appendix II. The

FIG. 6. — MEAN LENGTH OF SENTENCE IN WORDS FOR CHILDREN FROM THE SIX OCCUPATIONAL GROUPS

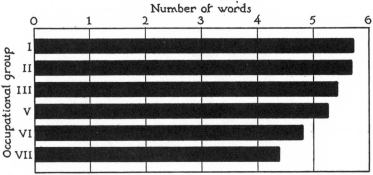

mean length of response is shown graphically in Figure 6. The distribution by sentence length throughout the occupational categories is by no means uniform for the sexes. The average decrease in sentence length from Group I to Group VII for 5½-year-old girls is about five times as great as that for 5½-year-old boys. In the 6½-year group the mean for boys from Group VII is greater than that for boys from Group I, but for girls there is a decrease of 1.23 words, which is about 22 per cent of the mean length for all 6½-year-old girls. At 9½, on the other hand, the mean decrease

TABLE 13. — RELATION BETWEEN MEAN NUMBER OF WORDS PER
REMARK AND RATING ON BEHAVIOR SCALES *

AGE IN YEARS	GROUP RATING I		GROUP RATING 2 OR 3		CRITICAL RATIO
	Length of Sentence	Number of Cases	Length of Sentence	Number of Cases	
Shyness					
5½	5.00	181	3.50	67	7.30
6½	5.63	41	4.53	22	3.50
9½	7.00	96	5.00	29	4.02
Negativism					
5½	4.65	233	3.27	15	3.83
6½	5.50	56	3.52	7	....
9½	6.67	119	4.08	6	....
Distractibility					
5½	4.49	226	5.34	22	2.83
6½	5.15	56	6.32	7	....
9½	6.55	124	5.48	1	....

* For a description of the behavior scales see page 25 and Appendix III.

TABLE 14. — RELATION BETWEEN MEAN NUMBER OF WORDS PER
REMARK AND OCCUPATIONAL STATUS OF PARENT

GROUP	NUMBER OF CASES	MEAN LENGTH OF REMARK		
		Boys	Girls	Both
5½ years				
Upper occupational	117	4.57	5.04	4.81
Lower occupational	131	4.44	4.27	4.35
Both	248	4.50	4.64	4.57
6½ years				
Upper occupational	31	5.39	5.77	5.58
Lower occupational	32	4.80	5.20	4.99
Both	63	5.07	5.49	5.28
9½ years				
Upper occupational	60	6.93	6.80	6.87
Lower occupational	65	5.92	6.57	6.25
Both	125	6.41	6.68	6.55
All ages				
Upper occupational	208	5.38	5.66	5.51
Lower occupational	228	4.90	5.06	4.98
Both	436	5.13	5.35	5.24

for boys is 3.07 words, or 47.9 per cent of the mean for all 9½-year-old boys, while for girls there is an increase of .63 words.

The results of the analysis for length of sentence were compared with the findings obtained by the scales for rating behavior. Apparently shy and negativistic children tend to use short sentences, while distractible children tend to use long sentences. The value of these findings, which are summarized in Table 13, is of course materially lessened by the fact that the examiner herself made the ratings, and was undoubtedly influenced by the child's readiness to talk.

TABLE 15. — MEAN NUMBER OF WORDS PER REMARK MADE BY CHILDREN FROM UPPER AND LOWER OCCUPATIONAL GROUPS

Group	Twins			Singletons			Only Children		
	Boys	Girls	Both	Boys	Girls	Both	Boys	Girls	Both
5½ years									
Upper occupational	4.71	4.68	4.69	4.23	4.98	4.60	4.96	5.82	5.39
Lower occupational	4.31	4.13	4.22	4.62	3.90	4.25	4.37	5.27	4.81
Both	4.48	4.39	4.43	4.43	4.40	4.41	4.65	5.55	5.09
6½ years									
Upper occupational	5.80	5.95	5.87	4.85	5.16	5.00	5.51	6.32	5.91
Lower occupational	5.19	4.76	4.97	4.55	5.69	5.12	4.62	5.26	4.90
Both	5.47	5.30	5.39	4.69	5.40	5.04	5.07	5.85	5.44
9½ years									
Upper occupational	7.40	7.21	7.30	6.65	6.24	6.44	6.57	7.13	6.85
Lower occupational	5.28	4.94	5.11	5.49	7.60	6.54	8.20	7.31	7.72
Both	6.34	6.07	6.20	6.03	6.97	6.50	7.38	7.23	7.30
All ages									
Upper occupational	5.70	5.59	5.64	5.02	5.37	5.19	5.47	6.25	5.86
Lower occupational	4.69	4.45	4.57	4.88	5.22	5.05	5.34	5.86	5.60
Both	5.15	5.00	5.07	4.95	5.29	5.12	5.41	6.06	5.73

In Table 14, boys and girls from the upper occupational group are compared at each age with boys and girls from the lower occupational group. The mean length of remark is appreciably greater for children from the upper occupational group, but in no case is the difference quite large enough to satisfy the criterion for statistical reliability. Girls use slightly longer sentences than boys, although the difference is not reliable, and the difference favors the boys very slightly in the case of the lower section of the 5½-year group and the upper section of the 9½-year group. There is a fairly uniform increase in sentence length with advancing age.

DIFFERENCES IN SENTENCE LENGTH BETWEEN TWINS, SINGLETONS, AND ONLY CHILDREN

Further differences in length of sentence appear when twins are compared with the singletons and only children at each age level. This is done in Table 15. These data indicate that twins of the ages included in this study use sentences equal in length to those of the singletons with siblings, but not equal to those used by the only child. Closer scrutiny, however, reveals the probability that twins of the lower occupational group still retain the shorter sentence

TABLE 16. — CRITICAL RATIOS BETWEEN VARIOUS SUBGROUPS
FOR MEAN SENTENCE LENGTH

Groups Compared	Critical Ratio
Boys of 5½ and 6½	2.29
Boys of 6½ and 9½	3.67 *
Boys of 5½ and 9½	5.97 *
Girls of 5½ and 6½	3.03 *
Girls of 6½ and 9½	2.85
Girls of 5½ and 9½	5.86 *
All children 5½ and all 6½	3.74 *
All children 6½ and all 9½	4.25 *
Boys and girls of 5½	0.79
Boys and girls of 6½	1.32
Boys and girls of 9½	0.59
All boys and all girls	1.17
Upper-class boys and girls of 5½	1.92
Upper- and lower-class girls of 5½	2.89
All upper- and all lower-class children of 5½	2.59
All upper- and all lower-class boys	1.92
All upper- and all lower-class girls	2.14
All upper- and all lower-class children	2.84
All upper-class boys and girls	1.00
All lower-class boys and girls	0.64
Upper- and lower-class twin girls of 5½	1.45
Upper- and lower-class singleton girls of 5½	2.51
Upper- and lower-class twin girls of 9½	2.01
Upper- and lower-class twin boys of 9½	2.75
All upper- and all lower-class twins	3.83 *
All twin and all singleton girls	0.87
All twin girls and all singleton and only girls	1.90
All twin and all only girls	2.81
All only girls and all twin and singleton girls	2.73
All only boys and all twin and singleton boys	1.06
All only upper-class boys and girls	1.20

* Starred critical ratios indicate significant differences.

which was characteristic of the preschool twin. The mean length of remark for twins from the upper occupational group tends to equal or exceed that of the singletons, and at 9½ even exceeds that of the only child; but this is by no means true of twins from the lower occupational group. This suggests that unless the environment is exceptionally good, twins are likely to retain the initial handicap which Day discovered. The difference in sentence length between all upper-class twins and all lower-class twins is statistically reliable (critical ratio 3.83). Group differences in length of remark are summarized in Table 16.

TABLE 17. — MEAN NUMBER OF WORDS PER REMARK AT DIFFERENT AGES, AS FOUND BY McCARTHY (80) AND BY DAVIS

Age in Years	Number of Cases	Boys	Girls	Both Sexes	SD	σ_m
		McCarthy				
3½	20	4.2	4.4	4.3	2.83	.09
4	20	4.3	4.4	4.4	2.86	.09
4½	20	4.6	4.7	4.6	2.95	.09
		Davis				
5½	248	4.5	4.6	4.6	1.41	.09
6½	63	5.1	5.5	5.3	1.37	.17
9½	125	6.4	6.7	6.5	2.30	.20

In Table 17, which is a continuation of the table given on page 54 of McCarthy's monograph, the increase in sentence length with advancing age is presented. Although there seems to be little or no increase in mean length of response between 3½ and 5½ years, nevertheless this conclusion may not be valid. In the first place, since McCarthy's work was based on only twenty subjects at each age level, sampling errors are not improbable; secondly, her study included no twins, who are markedly retarded in sentence length at precisely the ages under consideration; thirdly, about 20 per cent of her subjects were in the habit of associating mainly with adults, and these children, who were found to use longer sentences than the other subjects, may have been massed at these three age levels, since this factor was not controlled in selecting subjects; finally, it is possible that in the situation employed for the present study children tend to an undue proportion of monosyllabic and cryptic utterances.

The type of toys used proved eminently satisfactory in securing interest and cooperation and in minimizing shyness, but often the child's very absorption seemed to shorten the child's remarks and even to alter their functional make-up. Analysis of the records according to percentage distribution of remarks of each length yields a surprisingly high percentage of single-word responses — quite different from Stalnaker's (129) findings. Expletives are common, often accompanying difficulty in manipulating toys because of the animals' legs being bent, the table not being level, or a slight jar sending a whole encampment or parade to destruction. The writer is

TABLE 18. — MEAN NUMBER OF WORDS PER REMARK MADE BY TWINS, AS FOUND BY DAY (31) AND BY DAVIS

AGE IN YEARS	BOYS		GIRLS		BOTH SEXES	YEARLY INCREMENT
	Number	Mean Length	Number	Mean Length		
			Day			
2.	20	0.80	20	1.42	1.12	. . . .
3.	20	2.34	20	2.25	2.29	1.17
4.	19	2.93	21	2.92	2.92	0.63
5.	20	2.87	20	3.48	3.16	0.24
			Davis			
5½.	48	4.48	48	4.39	4.43	1.27 *
6½.	11	5.47	11	5.30	5.39	0.96
9½.	24	6.34	24	6.07	6.20	0.27 †

* Six months.   † Total increment for the three-year interval=0.81.

convinced that the data obtained underestimate rather than overestimate the length, type, and complexity of speech characteristic of children at the ages studied.

The probability that the inclusion of twins in the McCarthy study would have changed her findings may be demonstrated by the aid of a table published by Day. It is necessary, of course, to assume that the findings of Day and McCarthy are interchangeable, not an unwarrantable assumption in view of the fact that the two studies were carried on at the same institution with similar equipment and under the same direction. In the present study, 96 out of 248 cases at the 5½-year level were twins, and 152 were only children or singletons with siblings. That is, the number of twins is 63 per cent of the total number of singletons. The mean length of remark for twins at 48 months is 2.9 words; for singletons 4.4 words. If to the 20 children whose mean length of remark is 4.4 words we add 12 (63 per cent of 20) whose mean length of remark is 2.9 words, the mean for the 32 cases becomes 3.8 words. For a 4-year-old group so selected as to be comparable to the 5½-year-old group in the present study, it appears then that the true length of remark is 3.8 words, and the mean length of 4.6 words at 5½ years represents an appreciable increase.

A more satisfactory comparison may be made with twins alone, since in Day's data there is no complication resulting from the unknown proportion of only children. This comparison is made in Table 18. Here appreciable increments appear at each age, with the greatest difference at the point where the break occurs between the two studies.

The apparent spurt between 5 and 5½ years may be due to sampling, to differing technique in the two studies, to rapidly improving articulation on the part of twins at this period, or to the stimulation of the kindergarten environment. The sampling error, if present, is probably in the Day data, since she used only 20 pairs of twins at each year, while in the present study the 5½-year group contained 48 pairs.

Although the amount of increase in sentence length between the ages of 4 and 5½ years must remain problematical because of variations in technique, the increases between 5½ and 6½ years, and between 6½ and 9½ years, are statistically reliable. The critical ratio in the first instance is 3.74 and in the second instance 4.25. We may conclude that in similarly selected groups the mean length of remark continues to increase up to the age of 9½ years.

The mean length of sentence at 9½ years was found to be 6.55 words, an increase of 1.98 words over the mean of 4.57 words at 5½. Assuming that this increment is evenly spaced over the four-year span, it appears that the mean annual increase in sentence length throughout the early school period is 0.5 words. This seems to be a justifiable assumption because the mean increase between 5½ and 6½ years is .42 words, although the 6½-year group contains only 63 cases. On this basis let us compare the twins, singletons, and only children at the three age levels as to development in length of response. Table 19 shows the superiority of the singletons and only children over the twins. Apparently the twin boy does not suffer an appreciable handicap as compared with other boys in regard to increase in sentence length, but the twin girl is from 9 to 24 months retarded.

When the twins are compared with the singletons alone, no superiority is found for the singletons save for the 9½-year-old girls, where the difference amounts to .90 words, or 22 months of development. In all other instances the difference is negligible or even in favor of the twins. On the other hand, the only children are distinctly superior to both the twins and the singletons. (See Table 20.

TABLE 19. — AMOUNT OF SUPERIORITY OF SINGLETONS AND ONLY CHILDREN OVER TWINS IN MEAN LENGTH OF REMARK

MEASURE	5½-YEAR GROUP		6½-YEAR GROUP		9½-YEAR GROUP		ALL	
	Boys	Girls	Boys	Girls	Boys	Girls	Boys	Girls
Difference in number of words per remark.	.03	.40	..	.39	.11	.99	0	.56
Months of development represented by difference	1	10	..	9	3	24	0	13

TABLE 20. — AMOUNT OF SUPERIORITY OF ONLY CHILDREN OVER TWINS AND SINGLETONS IN MEAN LENGTH OF REMARK

MEASURE	5½-YEAR GROUP		6½-YEAR GROUP		9½-YEAR GROUP		ALL	
	Boys	Girls	Boys	Girls	Boys	Girls	Boys	Girls
Difference in number of words per remark.	.20	1.16	..	.50	1.20	.71	.31	.94
Months of development represented by difference	4	28	..	12	29	17	7	22

TABLE 21. — MEAN DECREASE IN LENGTH OF REMARK BETWEEN OCCUPATIONAL GROUPS I AND VII

GROUP	BOYS		GIRLS		BOTH SEXES	
	Number of Words	Percentage of Mean Length for Group	Number of Words	Percentage of Mean Length for Group	Number of Words	Percentage of Mean Length for Group
Twins	1.95	37.8	1.41	28.2	1.69	33.3
Singletons	.95	19.2	1.69	31.9	1.31	25.6
Only children. . .	....	....	1.35	22.3	.39	6.8

It appears that up to the age of 9½ years an environment which affords much association with adults favors the use of long sentences. This association seems to develop language maturity as measured by the mean length of remark to an amount equal in the case of boys to 7 months of chronological age, and in the case of girls to 22 months of chronological age. Twinship does not appear to be a greater handicap than the possession of ordinary siblings.

Twins, singletons, and only children tend to show the same decrease in sentence length between Group I and Group VII of the occupational categories that was found in the three age groups. The amount of decrease in sentence length between Group I and Group VII for twins, singletons, and only children is given in Table 21. The amount of decrease is greatest for the twins and strikingly least for the only children. In the case of only boys there is even an increase of .31 words, which is 5.7 per cent of the mean sentence length for only boys.

The same differences were shown above in Table 15, in which the mean length of remark for children from the three upper occupational classes was compared with that for children from the lower classes. For twins there is a difference of over a word in favor of children from the upper classes, but the corresponding differences for singletons and only children are negligible. In twins from both the upper and lower groups the mean length is greater for boys than for girls, a finding which is difficult to explain un-

FIG. 7. — INCREASE IN SENTENCE LENGTH FOR TWINS, SINGLETONS, AND ONLY CHILDREN FROM FIVE AND ONE-HALF TO NINE AND ONE-HALF YEARS

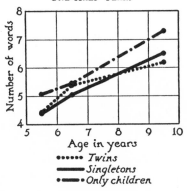

.... Twins
——— Singletons
•——• Only children

less it is due to the greater shyness of twin girls. The annual increase in sentence length for twins, singletons, and only children is shown graphically in Figure 7. Sex and occupational group differences are shown in Figure 8.

INTELLIGENCE AND SENTENCE LENGTH

Since it has been found that both intelligence and sentence length decrease as we go down the occupational scale, we should expect a

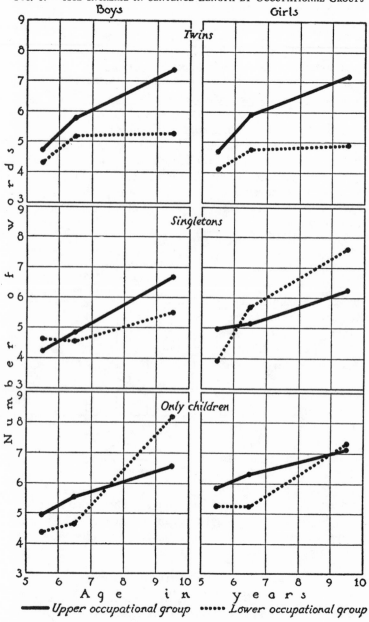

FIG. 8. — AGE INCREASE IN SENTENCE LENGTH BY OCCUPATIONAL GROUPS

Boys   Girls

Twins

Singletons

Only children

Number of words

Age in years

—— *Upper occupational group*   ••••• *Lower occupational group*

positive correlation between intelligence and sentence length. Day found that such a relationship existed for preschool twins. The coefficient (Pearsonian r) except at 4 years was .42 or .43, with a probable error of ±.09 to .11. At 4 years the relationship was —.07. In the present study the coefficient at 5½ years was .48±.03; at 6½ years .21±.08; and at 9½ years .20±.06.

There is a slight negative relationship between length of time and length of remark, indicating that the children who use longer sentences tend to make their fifty remarks in a shorter time. The coefficients are —.03±.04 at 5½ years; —.45±.07 at 6½ years; and —.12±.06 at 9½ years. McCarthy (79) noted the same tendency for children in the playground situation.

VARIABILITY IN LENGTH OF REMARK

Absolute variability. — Variability in length of remark was determined by two methods. The first procedure was to calculate the standard deviation of a distribution of the mean length of remarks for the children making up each group. The statement that the mean length of remark for children in the 5½-year group is 4.6 words with a standard deviation of 1.41 words indicates that at this age the mean length of response for 68.26 per cent of the children is between 3.2 and 6.0 words. The standard deviations given in Table 17 and used in obtaining the critical ratios listed in Table 16 were calculated in this way.

The procedure in the second instance involves the actual distribution of remarks for the individual children. The standard deviation for each child's mean length of remark was calculated, and group differences were brought out by computing the mean standard deviation for each group. A standard deviation of 2.62 words for a child whose mean sentence length is 5.26 words indicates that 68.26 per cent of that child's remarks are between 2.64 and 7.88 words.

Both methods indicate that variability in sentence length increases with age and is greater for girls than for boys, but the second method gives more striking group differences. The results are given in graphic form in Figure 9. This is the standard deviation used in calculating the coefficient of variability, which is described in the next section.

Individual variability is appreciably greater in both boys and girls from the upper occupational classes than in those from the

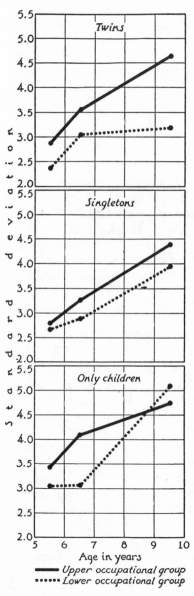

Standard deviation

Twins

Singletons

Only children

Age in years

—— *Upper occupational group*
•••••• *Lower occupational group*

lower occupational classes. Only children are more variable than twins and singletons. Only children from the lower occupational classes not only maintain their lead over twins and singletons from the lower classes, but at 9½ years actually forge ahead not only of twins and singletons from the upper classes but even of only children from the upper classes. Twins from the upper occupational classes at 5½ years are more variable than singletons of the same social background, and they maintain their lead up to 9½ years. Twins from the lower occupational classes, on the other hand, are not only less variable than singletons at the age of 5½ years but they increase in variability hardly at all. Since exactly the same characteristic was reported above for the mean length of sentence for twins from the lower occupational classes, we now have additional ground for believing that in an extremely favorable environment the language handicap of preschool twins is likely to disappear, but that otherwise it will persist at least well into the elementary school period.

Relative variability. — Since we are told (38) that comparisons based on absolute variability are often misleading, the coefficient of variability in sentence length for each child was computed, using the following formula, given by Garrett (38, page 41):

$$V = \frac{100\,SD}{m}.$$

It was found, however, that relating the standard deviation to the mean often gave an erroneous impression. This is clearly shown by considering the lower occupational group of 5½-year-old singletons, in which the boys were superior to the girls not only in length of

TABLE 22. — PERCENTAGE OF CHILDREN IN THE LOWER OCCUPATIONAL GROUPS WHO REACH OR EXCEED THE MEDIAN FOR THE UPPER GROUPS IN VARIABILITY OF SENTENCE LENGTH

Age in Years	Boys		Girls	
	SD	V	SD	V
5½.	43.9	43.9	30.8	53.8
6½.	23.5	41.2	33.3	40.0
9½.	25.0	53.1	39.4	39.4

TABLE 23. — PERCENTAGE OF BOYS WHO REACH OR EXCEED THE MEDIAN FOR GIRLS IN VARIABILITY OF SENTENCE LENGTH

Age in Years	Upper		Lower	
	SD	V	SD	V
5½.	36.2	46.5	45.4	36.4
6½.	40.0	53.2	47.0	52.9
9½.	43.3	36.6	31.2	25.0

sentence but in intelligence test scores. The mean length for boys was 4.62 words, but for girls only 3.90 words. The mean individual standard deviation for the boys of the group was 2.74 words, for the girls 2.58 words. If now we relate the standard deviation to the mean, the resulting coefficient of variability proves to be 61.4 for boys, 68.0 for girls. Consulting the individual data sheets, we find a girl whose V is 118.9. She used 37 single-word expressions, but since she also used one eight-word sentence, two nine-word sentences, and one eleven-word sentence, the V is extremely high. Her mean length of response was 1.90 words and her standard deviation 2.26 words. In another instance there were 41 single-word expressions, but a single seven-word sentence brought the V to 73.9.

In spite of the individual variations, the coefficient of variability follows the same general trends indicated by the absolute variability. V is greater for upper than for lower occupational groups and greater for only children than for twins and singletons. It increases somewhat with age, and is slightly greater for girls than for boys.

TABLE 24. — PERCENTAGE OF CHILDREN IN THE 5½-YEAR GROUP WHO REACH OR EXCEED THE MEDIAN FOR THE OLDER GROUPS IN VARIABILITY OF SENTENCE LENGTH

Sex	6½-Year Group		9½-Year Group	
	SD	V	SD	V
Boys	29.8	41.1	6.4	44.3
Girls	37.1	51.6	13.7	36.3

TABLE 25. — PERCENTAGE OF 5½-YEAR SUBGROUPS WHO REACH OR EXCEED THE MEDIAN FOR SPECIFIED 9½-YEAR SUBGROUPS IN VARIABILITY OF SENTENCE LENGTH

5½-Year Subgroups Equaling or Exceeding 9½-Year Subgroups	9½-Year Subgroups Equaled or Exceeded	SD	V
All girls	Boys	25.8	54.0
Upper-class boys	Lower-class boys	13.8	46.5
Upper-class girls	Lower-class girls	20.3	35.6
Only boys	Twin boys	7.4	44.4
Only boys	Singleton boys	7.4	44.4
Only girls	Twin girls	50.0	30.8
Only girls	Singleton girls	23.1	46.1
Only girls	Singleton boys	46.3	50.0
Only girls	Twin boys	50.0	63.1

The coefficient of variability has little relationship to intelligence. The Pearsonian r for 5½-year-old boys is —.06; for 5½-year-old girls —.12; for the 6½-year group .15 ±.08; and for the 9½-year group —.06.

Group comparisons of variability in terms of overlapping. — Group differences in variability of sentence length may be shown by computing the percentage of one group which reach or exceed the median of the other. This has been done using both the absolute and relative variability. There are some discrepancies in the results, although the general picture is the same. On the whole it appears that the effect of using the coefficient of variability is to decrease the differences, although there are exceptions. Upper and lower occupational groups are compared in Tables 22 and 23, and age groups in Table 24.

The effect of sex, social status, and sibling relationship on variability of sentence length may be further indicated by computing the percentage of a superior group who reach or exceed the median of an older, less favored group. In Table 25 the superior sections of the 5½-year group are compared with the inferior sections of the 9½-year group. Comparisons between twins, singletons, and only children are summarized in Table 26.

TABLE 26. — OVERLAPPING OF GROUPS IN MEASURES OF VARIABILITY

Group	Percentage Exceeding Median in SD	Percentage Exceeding Median in V
Twin boys reaching or exceeding median singleton boy. .	55.4	40.9
Twin boys reaching or exceeding median only boy. . . .	42.2	40.9
Singleton boys reaching or exceeding median only boy . .	36.0	53.5
Twin girls reaching or exceeding median singleton girl . .	36.1	48.2
Twin girls reaching or exceeding median only girl	25.3	41.0
Singleton girls reaching or exceeding median only girl . .	33.7	43.7

DISTRIBUTION OF REMARKS ACCORDING TO LENGTH IN WORDS

The frequency with which sentences of various word lengths occur has been so little studied that except for Davis' (30) question study no data are available for comparison. No single-word questions were included in the questionnaire material on which the former study was based, because of the difficulty of interpreting such responses; consequently it is impossible to say whether the very large percentage of single-word expressions in the present study would be verified in another investigation. Probably the experimental material was partly responsible, since many expletives or one-word utterances resulted from the child's exasperation with a refractory toy or his preoccupation with his project.

For every group, at all ages, the curve follows the same general form. Approximately 19 per cent of all remarks are one word long. This is the high point for each group, and in every instance there is a sharp drop in the frequency of two-word remarks. A second peak occurs for four-word remarks; thereafter the curve drops rapidly for the younger children, gradually for the older ones, and tapers out very slowly. In the question study, the peak was at the five- and six-word point, but the three- and four-word point was not far behind for the younger group of children.

There are some minor but consistent group differences in the curves. The highest percentage of single-word utterances is found in the 5½-year group and the lowest in the 9½-year group. The youngest children use more two-, three-, four-, and five-word sentences, but the oldest group exceed them at each length thereafter. Among the 5½-year-old children there is a distinct difference in the percentage of one-word expressions between upper- and lower-class girls, although the curves for upper- and lower-class boys at this age are indistinguishable. Only 17.1 per cent of responses of upper-class girls are one word in length, but 26.7 per cent of the responses of lower-class girls are single words. For boys the corresponding percentages are 19.0 and 20.6. The inferiority of the lower-class girls is surprisingly constant as soon as the three-word sentence is reached. Thereafter the curves for upper and lower groups are similar in contour, with that for the upper girls uniformly higher.

In the 9½-year group this difference between upper- and lower-class girls largely disappears. The percentage of single-word remarks is slightly greater for girls in the upper group; the lower group exceed the upper in percentage of five-, six-, seven-, eight-, nine-, and ten-word responses, and thereafter the curves practically coincide. Among boys at this age, on the other hand, 11.5 per cent of the remarks made by the upper group are one word long; 16.1 per cent are of this length in the lower group. The lower group exceed the upper in percentage of two-, three-, four-, and five-word responses, but thereafter the upper group is superior.

Singleton children give the greatest number of single-word responses; twins make more two-, three-, four-, and five-word remarks. The curve for only children runs below those for twins and singletons up to seven words, but thereafter at each length the percentage is greatest for the only children.

At 5½ and 9½ years there is a decided tendency for boys to use more three-, four-, five-, and six-word remarks than girls, but thereafter the girls consistently exceed the boys. At both ages the girls make more single-word responses. The 6½-year-old boys make more single-word responses than the girls, but drop below the girls in their use of two-, three-, and four-word remarks. They exceed the girls in use of five and six words, but thereafter the superiority is slightly in favor of the girls. Because of the fewer cases in this group, these findings of course are not so conclusive as those obtained for the other two groups.

It appears that children who exceed the average of their group in mean length of sentence tend to make few single-word and short remarks and many long ones.* Girls, however, make more single-word responses than boys, and we may look to this fact as well as to the greater number of long sentences for an explanation of the uniformly greater variability of girls. But it is noteworthy that these tendencies are never sufficient to displace the one- and four-word remarks from first and second place, respectively, in point of frequency.

Because of the great importance of single-word responses, a detailed analysis of their function will be presented in the following chapter.

Summary

1. The mean length of remark increases with age up to 9½ years.

2. It is slightly greater for girls than for boys.

3. Children from the upper occupational groups make longer remarks than children from the lower occupational groups. This difference is greater than the sex difference. At 5½ years the girls from the lower occupational groups make shorter remarks than the boys, but at 9½ years it is the boys from the lower occupational groups who tend to use short sentences.

4. The mean length of remark for twins at each age is approximately equal to that of singletons with siblings but is decidedly below that of only children. The performance of twins from the lower occupational groups however is not equal to that of the corresponding singletons, and the difference in sentence length between upper- and lower-class twins is statistically reliable. At each age twin boys use longer sentences than twin girls.

5. When the performance of twins is compared with that of both only children and singletons with siblings, it appears that twin boys are not appreciably inferior, but that twin girls are from 9 to 24 months retarded.

6. At each age children who were rated 1 for shyness used longer sentences than children who were rated 2 or 3, and the differences are statistically reliable.

7. Children rated 1 for negativism used longer sentences than

---

* For a discussion of the characteristics of these long sentences, see E. A. Davis, "Mean Sentence Length Compared with Long and Short Sentences as a Reliable Measure of Language Development," *Child Development*, 8: 69–79 (March, 1937).

children rated 2 or 3. The difference is statistically reliable at 5½ years, but because of the few cases involved the computation was not made for the older groups.

8. Children rated 1 for distractibility used shorter sentences than those rated 2 or 3.

9. Variability of sentence length increases with age and is greater for girls than for boys, and greater for children from upper than from lower occupational groups.

10. About 20 per cent of all remarks were one word in length. Girls use more single-word expressions than boys, but they also use more long remarks, while the remarks of boys tend to cluster at three, four, five, and six words. Only children use more very long sentences than do other children.

V. FUNCTIONAL ANALYSIS

METHOD OF ANALYSIS

The Piaget-McCarthy scheme of functional analysis proved usable for the subjects employed in this study, although the greater complexity of response necessitated further elaboration and subdivision of the category of "naming" if adequate differentiation were to be obtained. Seven subheads were distinguished, one of which, "judgment and deduction," finally absorbed the category of "criticism" used by Piaget (102) and McCarthy (80). The proper classification of the remark "This one falls down" proved by all odds the most troublesome point which came up in the course of the analysis. Is the child describing a situation or criticizing the object with ideas of reference? The decision is a nice one, and not unimportant, for because of the delicate manipulation involved in handling the toys, the remark appears with comparative frequency. The classification was made according to context and intonation. If an element of criticism appeared to be present, the remark was considered a judgment, otherwise a description. Such error as may have resulted is probably negligible, since both the categories concerned are among the more important ones, and about equally so.

The outline employed, with illustrations and empirical rules, was as follows:

I. Egocentric speech
   A. Repetition or echolalia
      Includes repetition of words or phrases used by examiner or child, for no apparent reason, or of rhymes or songs.
   B. Monologue
      1. Talking to self as though thinking aloud.
         Includes sighing and mannerisms such as murmuring "Let's see" without an amplifying remark.
      2. Humming
      3. Collective monologue
         No remarks were classified under this heading because the decision as to the part played by the adult's presence is a subjective one. Practically all remarks which Piaget would have placed under this heading have been classed as description. The clearly egocentric remarks were found to be

so very few that all have been classified under the comprehensive heading of egocentric speech.

II. Socialized speech
  A. Adapted information
    1. Classification and valuation
      a. Naming (unaccompanied by a modifier)
        Examples: "This is an Indian."
                 "Looks like an axe."
      b. Quantitative discrimination
        Examples: "Here's one."
                 "Two Indians now."
                 "You've got a lot of 'em."
      c. Part-whole relationship and ownership
        Examples: "There's what you pull it with."
                 "He's got a lasso."
                 "He's lost his arm."
      d. Discrimination, comparison, choice
        Examples: "These two are just alike."
                 "I like this kind best."
                 "This one is bigger."
      e. Classification and identification
        Includes naming accompanied by modifying word, phrase, or clause.
        Examples: "Another Indian."
                 "Here's a little pig."
                 "Indian shooting."
      (Omission of "is" places many remarks here which would otherwise belong under description.)
      f. Judgment and deduction
        Includes criticism, statement of knowledge or opinion, generalization, and interpretation. Expressions of liking and desire, placed by McCarthy under emotionally toned responses, have been considered in their intellectual rather than their emotional aspect, and classified here. Decisions and exceptions are included under this heading, and remarks introduced by such expressions as "he has to," "it needs," "he wants," "I think," "I guess," "I wonder," "I bet."
        Examples: "This has to go here."
                 "All the trees go over here."
                 "No, these are out in the farm."
                 "I don't know what this is."
                 "That is what I wanted to do."
                 "I'd like to keep 'em."

g. Definition
 Example: "Head cheese is plain meat, isn't it?"
2. Remarks about the immediate situation
 Includes descriptions of actions or intentions of self, experimenter, or toys.
 Examples: "Then this one comes galloping up."
 "These two are having a race now."
 "And then they saw trees, and off they bounded."
 "I'll take this one next."
 "Here goes a sheep."
 "Now he's shooting downward."
3. Remarks associated with the immediate situation
 Examples: "I go downstairs that way sometimes" (like the crawling Indian).
 "I used to have some Indians like these."
4. Remarks associated with conversation
 These are not elicited, since the examiner's remark is neither a question nor a command, and response is entirely optional. In a sense these remarks are a part of the immediate situation, but it seemed worth while to keep them distinct in order to have a measure of the total amount of verbal stimulation employed in obtaining the child's responses. When the examiner said, "I wonder if you play with toys like these at home," or "It's time to put them away now," one child would acknowledge the remark by a nod, another by a monosyllable, and a third by a torrent of conversation. When this occurred, the first remark alone was classified as associated with conversation and subsequent ones as associated with the situation. Sometimes the examiner, busy with recording, paused midway in answering the child's question, and the remark was finished by the child. Such instances are included here, as are single repetitions of a remark of the examiner, since these, being clearly associated with the situation and arising from conversation, do not meet the criterion for egocentricity laid down above.
 Example: S. What's he got?
 E. A tomahawk.
 S. A tomahawk.
 Instead of repeating the examiner's response, the child might object, "But it looks like an axe." This remark in such a situation would be classified here, although if it occurred without any conversation on the part of the examiner it would be considered naming.

This type of remark seems to be frequent with children who are at ease with adults and converse freely, and also with those who are taciturn or ill at ease, but have learned that some verbal response to adults' remarks is expected. In the latter case these responses are only one step removed from the category of answers.

5. Irrelevant remarks
Includes all irrelevant remarks, even though the second or third such remark is logically related to the first.

B. Incomplete responses
Includes fragmentary or incomprehensible remarks.

C. Emotionally toned remarks
This category has been limited to exclamations such as "Gee!" "For the land's sake!" "Will you look at that!" and to definite commands. If "H'm!" is uttered with marked astonishment, or "There!" with clear satisfaction, the response is considered emotionally toned.

D. Questions
An interrogative phrase tacked on to a declarative sentence is not classified as a question; but a sentence begun as a question, left unfinished, and completed in declarative form *is* classified as a question.

"Is it — this is a real Indian."

If a child replies to a question by asking another because he has not understood or because he desires greater precision, the question is classified as a question and the next remark as an answer.

Example: E. What does your Daddy do?
S. Mean when he's working?
E. Yes.
S. He works in electric machinery.

E. Answers
"Answers to real questions and commands." This includes all elicited responses.

F. Social phrases
Examples: "Thank you."
"Excuse me."
"You're welcome."

G. Dramatic imitation, including imaginative play.
Examples: "Hello, pony."
"Now he shoots, bang! bang!"

Summary of method. — Certain changes have been made in McCarthy's scheme for functional analysis of responses. One important category, that of remarks associated with or arising out of conversation, has been added; criticism has been absorbed by one subhead of naming, and data have been made available as to the prevalence of counting, comparison, and definition. Since many of McCarthy's remarks about the immediate situation would fall under these heads, direct comparison with the McCarthy and Day findings for some categories will be impossible. By including her percentage classified as criticism with the total percentage of adapted information, however, and adding all the subheads distinguished in the above analysis together, a fairly satisfactory approximation may be made.

Results

Adapted information and criticism. — In McCarthy's 4½-year group, 55.3 per cent of the remarks were classified under adapted information and criticism. The corresponding percentages for the subjects in the present study were 59.7 at 5½ years, 66.8 at 6½, and 60.7 at 9½ years.

At all these ages a large and fairly constant percentage of all conversation falls under the general heads of "naming" and "remarks about or associated with the situation," first distinguished by McCarthy (80). There is a suggestion of a small but steady increase with age in the percentage of such remarks for boys, but decided fluctuation for girls.

Answers. — McCarthy found the percentage of "answers" increasingly important in her two upper age groups. In the present study "answers" comprise the largest single category, and the percentage is markedly higher at 9½ than at 5½ years. We do not know whether this results from mental growth or from adaptation to school and social situations. There is a slight positive correlation at each age between the number of spontaneous remarks and IQ. The Pearsonian r at 5½ years is $.19\pm.04$; at 6½ years $.12\pm.08$; and at 9½ years $.16\pm.06$. This would cause us to expect the percentage of answers to decrease with age, and would lend weight to explanation in terms of personality and school training.

Greater spontaneity of speech is unquestionably characteristic of boys. McCarthy found 3.7 per cent of answers among her girls of 18 months, but none among the boys, and thereafter the percentage is higher for the girls at each age except 48 months. In the present study the difference appears to a marked degree except in the small 6½-year group. McCarthy found answers more important in the upper occupational group up to the age of 30 months; the groups were equal at 36 and 42 months; but at 48 and 54 months the ratio changed. In the present study the percentage of answers is uniformly higher for the children in the lower occupational group, although the difference decreases with age.

It is probable that this finding may be explained by known facts as to the differing development and socialization of the sexes and by differences in the handling of young children in the two strata of society. In the poorer homes little conversation is addressed to the very young child, and such remarks as he makes are spontaneous.

TABLE 27. — MEAN PERCENTAGES OF ANSWERS IN TOTAL REMARKS, AS FOUND BY McCARTHY (80) AND BY DAVIS

Group	McCARTHY (4 and 4½ years)	DAVIS		
		5½ years	6½ years	9½ years
Boys				
Upper occupational	. . . .	15.8	15.7	23.3
Lower occupational	. . . .	22.0	21.9	27.6
Both	27.5	19.1	19.0	25.5
Girls				
Upper occupational	. . . .	17.2	16.1	39.9
Lower occupational	. . . .	30.8	21.9	39.6
Both	30.5	24.3	18.9	39.8
Both sexes				
Upper occupational	24.2	16.5	15.9	31.3
Lower occupational	32.3	26.4	21.2	33.7
Both	29.0	21.7	18.9	32.7

As he grows older this spontaneity is not encouraged, and he tends more and more to occupy himself in silence, speaking only when a definite need arises. In the better type of home, where there is more space and adults have more leisure, both the social type of conversation and the apparently purposeless but actually teleological chatter are encouraged. But in the school situation spontaneous conversation must be somewhat curbed, and as time goes on the percentage of answers increases. Thus Zyve (163) noted that as her daily conversation periods progressed, the shy child talked more and the talkative child less. The higher percentage of answers for girls may be at the start an indication of the more rapid linguistic development of girls, but at the later ages probably is due to a great extent to the greater tractability of girls in all social situations. That differential treatment for the sexes obtains in the poorer home seems very probable when boys and girls are considered separately at the various ages. (See Table 27.)

The marked difference in spontaneity of response between 5½-year-old girls of the upper and lower occupational groups is in keeping with what was found in regard to shyness and sentence length. When twins are compared with the other children in percentage of answers, this is found to be less than the percentage of judgments for twin and only boys, and of equal rank with judgments for only girls. At the two earlier age levels the percentage of answers is strikingly small for only girls as compared with twin and singleton girls. There is little difference in boys, although at all ages twin and only boys show greater readiness of response than do single-

TABLE 28. — MEAN PERCENTAGE OF ANSWERS IN TOTAL REMARKS MADE
BY TWINS, SINGLETONS, AND ONLY CHILDREN

AGE IN YEARS	TWINS			SINGLETONS			ONLY		
	Boys	Girls	Both	Boys	Girls	Both	Boys	Girls	Both
5½	18.8	24.8	21.8	20.6	30.3	25.5	16.7	12.1	14.4
6½	16.9	20.7	18.8	22.0	23.4	22.7	18.0	11.1	14.7
9½	15.5	44.2	29.8	38.4	35.8	37.1	17.7	39.5	29.1

tons, with a striking difference at 9½ years. At this age the percentage of answers is extremely high for all girls, but it is difficult to understand why singleton boys of 9½ should employ 38 per cent answers, while twin and only boys have a percentage of about 17. It is possible that only boys of this age are more at ease in the presence of a strange woman than are singleton boys with siblings, and that any embarrassment felt by twin boys is offset when they learn of the examiner's interest in twins; but why do twin girls, given exactly the same explanation, show such reluctance at entering into conversation? The percentages of answers recorded for the several groups are presented in Table 28.

Because of its numerical importance, a detailed analysis of the category of answers was undertaken. It was found that most of the remarks included were exactly what is generally understood by the term, complete and definite answers to questions or commands. If the examiner asked, "What is this?" the child usually named the object; if she asked, "What is he doing?" the action was described. If the question took the form, "Why did the pioneers use oxen to pull the wagons instead of horses?" the child would offer some explanation. Answers of this type could undoubtedly be classified according to the functional scheme used for other types of response.

A total of 4,323, or 81.2 per cent of the 5,326 answers, were found to be answers in this sense. The percentage was slightly higher at 9½ than at 5½, and was noticeably lower at 6½, but because of the few cases at this age we are not warranted in drawing conclusions from this fact. There seems at each age to be a slight tendency toward a higher percentage of this type of answer for children in the lower occupational group. At 5½ and 6½ years the percentage is slightly higher for girls than for boys, but there is no difference at 9½.

Although the examiner was extremely careful to couch her questions and commands in such terms as to require more than the simple "yes" or "no" answer, the children showed themselves to be amazingly ingenious in finding opportunity for such expressions. The number of such answers is probably connected with general talkativeness. The taciturn or negativistic child would go out of his way to avail himself of the monosyllabic grunt expressing affirmation, negation, or acquiescence, while the talkative youngster even if he desired to convey such meanings would amplify his "yes," "sure," "all right," by qualifying phrases or clauses.

Figures given by Smith (122) and by Rugg, Krueger, and Sondergaard (111) indicate that the writer was more successful than they in avoiding the "yes" and "no" response. Stevenson (132) suggests that because of the difficulty of pronouncing "yes" and because of its diversity of application, the young child is likely to avoid its use, resorting to circumlocutions such as "it is" and "it does." The total frequency for "yes" in this study is 426, of "no," 399; and when "uh-huh" and "anh-anh" are added, we find 913 expressions of affirmation as compared with 594 expressions of denial. Analysis by age groups shows that at 9½ years children use both "yes" and "no" appreciably more than younger children, whose affirmations and denials are more often expressed by "uh-huh" or "anh-anh." Apparently Stevenson's theory, if true, applies only to preschool children.

These gradations of expression have all been distinguished in the scheme of classification which was employed. Although the percentages for all these minor categories of answers are small, some interesting age differences emerge. Thus at 5½ and 6½ years the simple affirmative usually takes the form of "uh-huh," "yeah," "eyah," and the simple negative is likely to be "anh-anh," "unh-hm," or some such unmistakable but orthographically complicated expression. At 9½ years these word forms are rare, but the simple "yes" and "no" comprise 8.8 per cent of all the answers. The disappearance of the childish expression and the substitution of "yes" and "no" are probably the result of school experience. The total use of the simple affirmative and negative was 13.1 per cent of answers at 5½, 25.8 per cent at 6½, and 10.3 per cent at 9½ years.

Expressions of acquiescence ("all right"), agreement, or indecision ("well — ") were rare at all ages. "I don't know" was somewhat important (3.6 per cent of all answers) at 5½ years, but became less frequent with age, while expressions of certainty or confirmation ("sure," "of course," "I know it") were infrequent at all ages.

Questions.—McCarthy found questions more frequent in girls up to 36 months and thereafter more frequent in boys, but in the present study the percentage is always higher for boys. At 5½ years the percentage is practically that which McCarthy found at 4 years; it is slightly less at 6½, and much less at 9½ years. Age differences are presented in Table 29.

Table 29 shows that, as during the preschool years, children from the upper occupational classes ask more questions than children from the lower classes, but by 9½ years the difference disappears. Nor is it as striking at 5½ and 6½ as at the earlier ages. Only children tend to ask rather more questions than twins and singletons. (See Table 30.)

TABLE 29. — MEAN PERCENTAGES OF QUESTIONS IN TOTAL REMARKS, AS FOUND BY McCARTHY (80) AND BY DAVIS

	McCARTHY (4 and 4½ years)		DAVIS		
GROUP			5½ years	6½ years	9½ years
Boys					
Upper occupational	....	....	14.0	19.5	4.6
Lower occupational	....	....	11.1	6.1	5.0
Both	12.8	10.1	12.5	12.4	4.8
Girls					
Upper occupational	....	....	12.3	10.1	2.7
Lower occupational	....	....	10.2	4.8	3.9
Both	11.5	5.8	11.2	7.5	3.3
Both sexes					
Upper occupational	....	....	13.1	14.6	3.7
Lower occupational	....	....	10.7	5.5	4.4
Both	12.1	8.2	11.8	10.0	4.1

The tendency for frequency of questions to decrease with age and to be greater for boys and for only children appears in the percentage of records on which questions are found, as well as in the mean number asked. Although girls are more likely than boys to ask no questions at all, the total variability in number of questions seems to be slightly greater for girls. In no case were there more than 26 questions on a boy's record, but one twin girl of 5½ asked 38 questions.

The coefficient of correlation (Pearson product-moment method) for the 5½-year group between intelligence as measured by the Pintner-Cunningham Test and number of questions asked in the

TABLE 30. — MEAN PERCENTAGE OF QUESTIONS IN TOTAL REMARKS MADE
BY TWINS, SINGLETONS, AND ONLY CHILDREN

Age	Twins			Singletons			Only Children		
	Boys	Girls	Both	Boys	Girls	Both	Boys	Girls	Both
5½	12.0	12.2	12.1	11.6	9.6	10.6	14.8	12.2	13.6
6½	14.6	6.4	10.5	10.8	8.0	9.4	11.6	8.4	10.0
9½	5.8	3.4	4.6	4.2	3.4	3.8	4.2	2.8	3.5

controlled situation set up in the present study was found to be —.04. Although the percentage of questions is decidedly less for the 9½-year group than for the younger children, we need further investigation before concluding that this decline results from a decrease in curiosity. Although it was a departure from school routine, the situation under which the records were obtained was a very simple one for the older children, and not likely to arouse a desire for information. Moreover, we should expect children, as their remarks become less spontaneous with advancing age, to ask fewer questions; and in general we find that the order of frequency for questions is the reverse of that for answers.

The total of 2,037 questions on the 436 records seemed a large enough sampling to warrant analysis according to Piaget's (102) method as modified by Davis (30). In Davis' previous study of children's questions, lists were obtained and sent in by parents. The questions were asked under a wide variety of situations, and of all sorts of persons, by children varying widely in age and representing only the upper occupational groups. For all these reasons a comparison between the results of the questionnaire study and questions asked in a standardized situation by children at discrete ages and representative of the general population seemed well worth while.

In the former study, age differences were brought out by a rough division into a younger and an older group, but no attempt was made to establish distinct age levels. The mean age of children in the present study is 81.6 months, in the earlier study, 70.0 months. In comparing the findings, only one minor change in the scheme of classification proved necessary. Mothers were told to omit all single-word questions, for the reason that in questionnaire material it would be impossible to classify expressions like "what?" and "huh?" without a mass of explanatory material. In the present study all such single-word questions are included, although in spite of the examiner's care in recording, 39 questions were so indefinite that when classification was attempted, a category of "indefinite questions" had to be made.

When these data are compared with those of the former study, certain differences are revealed. Questions of cause decrease with age, and are somewhat more common in boys than in girls. Questions dealing with reality and history are somewhat more numerous and questions dealing with actions and intentions somewhat less numerous than in the earlier study. For children from the upper occupational group the mean percentage of causal questions is very close to that found in the earlier study. The situation would, of course, tend to limit the latter type of questions to those concerning the examiner and to a few irrelevant questions about other persons, or hypothetical ones involving pioneers and Indians suggested by the toys. Similarly we should expect the category of social relations to be of less importance than in situations where the children were engaged in actual everyday domestic relationships. We do find this, but questions of social relations are more common in the 9½-year group than among the younger children. Questions of classification proved by far the most important at all ages and for both sexes. The percentage is almost twice as great as that found in the earlier study. Questions of calculation are less frequent than in the earlier study, while rhetorical and indefinite questions are of very little importance. The distribution among the various categories is given in Table 31.

Emotionally toned remarks. — Emotionally toned remarks were of decreasing importance in McCarthy's older groups, dropping from 15 to 18 per cent at the early ages to 6.5 and 6.4 per cent at 48 and 54 months. The same trend was found in the present study up to 9½ years, at which age the percentage is only 1.8.

Girls in these age groups made more emotionally toned remarks than boys, whereas McCarthy found that up to the age of 4½ years the percentage was decidedly higher for boys. The fact that some responses classified as emotional by McCarthy are here considered as judgments or choices may have influenced the findings, although there seems to be no reason why more such remarks should be found in the conversation of boys than of girls. Probably during

TABLE 31. — PERCENTAGE DISTRIBUTION OF DIFFERENT TYPES OF QUESTIONS IN UPPER AND LOWER OCCUPATIONAL GROUPS

Group	Causality	Reality	Actions	Social Relations	Classification	Calculation	Rhetorical	Indefinite
Boys of 5½								
Upper occupational	15.0	24.4	16.2	1.2	40.6	1.0	0.0	1.5
Lower occupational	6.8	24.2	21.5	1.3	41.3	2.2	0.5	2.2
Girls of 5½								
Upper occupational	12.4	22.0	22.3	1.4	36.5	1.9	0.5	1.9
Lower occupational	9.3	16.5	23.1	4.5	43.5	0.0	0.0	3.0
Boys of 6½								
Upper occupational	7.5	24.0	21.2	2.7	38.3	2.7	0.0	3.4
Lower occupational	5.9	19.6	21.6	3.9	43.1	2.0	2.0	2.0
Girls of 6½								
Upper occupational	4.9	25.9	28.4	3.7	34.6	2.5	0.0	0.0
Lower occupational	5.5	22.2	22.2	2.8	36.1	0.0	11.1	0.0
Boys of 9½								
Upper occupational	4.3	18.8	34.8	7.2	34.8	0.0	0.0	0.0
Lower occupational	7.5	17.5	16.2	17.5	37.5	1.2	0.0	2.5
Girls of 9½								
Upper occupational	5.1	20.5	5.1	25.6	43.6	0.0	0.0	0.0
Lower occupational	3.1	23.4	29.7	12.5	31.2	0.0	0.0	0.0
All boys								
Upper occupational	12.1	23.7	19.5	2.2	39.4	1.3	0.0	1.8
Lower occupational	6.8	22.6	20.6	4.3	40.9	2.0	0.6	2.2
All girls								
Upper occupational	10.5	22.5	22.7	3.7	36.8	1.8	0.4	1.4
Lower occupational	8.1	18.0	24.0	5.5	41.1	0.0	0.9	2.3

the early years boys use more emotional verbalisms, just as they indulge more often than girls in overt expressions of anger. To what extent the greater difficulty experienced by boys in making themselves understood is a factor we do not know. It may be that in the present study boys made fewer emotionally toned remarks because of their absorption in the situation, or that school experience operated to reduce the number of such expressions.

There were more emotionally toned remarks in McCarthy's

upper than in her lower occupational group at 18 months, but thereafter the percentages were almost the same until at 48 and 54 months more such remarks were found among the lower group. In the present study the percentage is slightly greater for the upper group at all ages.

Day's (31) twins made many more emotionally toned remarks than did singletons of the same age. In the present study the twins at all ages and of both sexes are very similar to the singletons, but it is the only children who are most given to this type of response. (See Table 32.)

Naming and classification. — The naming category as defined for the purposes of this study was somewhat more important for younger than for older children, and more important for the lower

TABLE 32. — MEAN PERCENTAGES OF TOTAL REMARKS WHICH WERE
EMOTIONALLY TONED

AGE IN YEARS	TWINS		SINGLETONS		ONLY CHILDREN	
	Number of Cases	Percentage of Total Remarks	Number of Cases	Percentage of Total Remarks	Number of Cases	Percentage of Total Remarks
5½	96	4.2	99	3.8	53	5.8
6½	22	3.0	22	3.3	19	3.8
9½	48	1.6	52	1.4	25	3.0

than for the upper occupational groups. The percentage was slightly less for only children than for twins and singletons. There were individual children for whom naming was the principal type of response, probably because shyness prevented free conversation or because of difficulty with enunciation. The percentage of naming responses for only boys of 5½ in the lower occupational group was 11.4, yet there were very few instances of naming except on the records of two boys, of whom one had a severe speech defect, while the other displayed no interest in the toys but great enthusiasm in distinguishing the various types of ships in a book which he was shown. Among twin boys of 9½ in the lower occupational group the high percentage is due to the 27 naming responses of a subnormal boy who had been given a number of mental tests and seemed to consider that naming was expected of him (12 of his other responses were naming accompanied by a modifier and therefore came under classification); and to the 17 naming responses of a boy who was a year and a half retarded in school. There was no correlation at 5½ years between naming and intelligence (Pearsonian $r = -.02$), and observations of the children's behavior would support the conclusion that a high percentage of naming results from shyness or embarrassment at being misunderstood, rather than from immaturity. Sometimes the naming response seems to be a transition between answers and free conversation.

Classification seems to be approximately equal in importance

TABLE 33. — MEAN PERCENTAGES OF TOTAL REMARKS WHICH WERE
ASSOCIATED WITH THE SITUATION

AGE IN YEARS	TWINS			SINGLETONS			ONLY CHILDREN		
	Boys	Girls	Both	Boys	Girls	Both	Boys	Girls	Both
5½	2.6	2.4	2.5	3.0	5.0	4.0	4.2	6.0	5.0
6½	10.4	8.4	9.4	6.2	5.0	5.6	7.8	11.0	9.4
9½	3.4	2.6	3.0	8.0	6.0	7.0	5.4	7.8	6.8

TABLE 34. — MEAN PERCENTAGES OF TOTAL REMARKS WHICH WERE
STIMULATED BY CONVERSATION

AGE IN YEARS	TWINS			SINGLETONS			ONLY CHILDREN		
	Boys	Girls	Both	Boys	Girls	Both	Boys	Girls	Both
5½	3.6	4.4	4.0	6.8	5.6	6.2	7.8	6.6	7.2
6½	2.2	5.0	3.6	8.2	2.4	5.3	5.2	6.0	5.6
9½	6.0	5.2	5.6	7.6	5.2	6.4	7.6	7.6	7.6

to naming, but it is more nearly equal in frequency at all ages. The mean is 6.6 per cent at 5½ years, 7.4 per cent at 6½ years, and 8.2 at 9½ years. The mean percentage for boys is 8.4 and for girls 6.0.

Judgment. — Judgment is one of the most important categories for both boys and girls at all ages. The mean is 18.7 per cent for boys and 16.3 per cent for girls.

Other categories. — Description includes about 13 per cent of all responses for both boys and girls, with a slight increase at 9½ years. Remarks associated with the situation are summarized in Table 33.

Probably most of the responses classified as remarks stimulated by conversation would have been classified by McCarthy as associated with the situation. These are summarized in Table 34.

Since the categories of answers and remarks stimulated by conversation alike resulted from remarks of the examiner, it seemed advisable to compare the standing of groups in these two categories. No evidence was found which would indicate that children who did not require direct questioning from the examiner were receiving an undue amount of indirect impetus toward conversation from her general remarks. When the percentages of answers and remarks stimulated by conversation are combined as in Table 35, the trends are unaffected, indicating that for children who converse freely, remarks of the examiner are nonessential, while children who require the direct stimulation of questions also require the milder stimulation of desultory remarks. This bears out the examiner's impression.

TABLE 35. — MEAN PERCENTAGES OF TOTAL REMARKS WHICH RESULTED
FROM CONVERSATION OF THE EXAMINER

AGE IN YEARS	TWINS			SINGLETONS			ONLY CHILDREN		
	Boys	Girls	Both	Boys	Girls	Both	Boys	Girls	Both
5½	22.4	29.2	25.8	27.4	35.9	31.7	24.5	18.7	21.6
6½	19.1	25.7	22.4	30.2	25.8	28.0	23.2	17.1	20.3
9½	21.5	49.4	35.4	46.0	41.0	43.5	25.3	47.1	36.7

Irrelevant remarks made up 1.6 per cent of the remarks of 5½-year-old girls and 1.1 per cent of the remarks of 6½-year-old girls, but less than one per cent of the remarks of boys of the same ages. At 9½ years irrelevant remarks did not occur at all on the records of only children, and were very rare in twins and singletons.

Egocentric remarks.—The percentage of egocentric remarks in McCarthy's groups varied from 0.5 to 10.2. In general, the importance of this type of speech lessens with age, and the percentage of remarks classified as egocentric in the present study is very small. Most of the remarks so classified occurred under the circumstances which seemed conducive to emotionally toned remarks, namely, difficulty in making toys stand up. This finding is in keeping with the statement of Vygotsky and Luria (146) that egocentric speech appears when the child is confronted with a difficult situation and is trying to solve the problem verbally. They believe that in later life internal speech supplants this type of comment.

Social phrases. — This category, of little importance in preschool children, dwindles in older groups to infinitesimal proportions. This may be partly due to the situation, but it is possible that during the period of most rapid acquisition of speech such phrases are more often used than after they are mastered.

Dramatic imitation. — This is another small category, which in general seems to be somewhat more frequent in boys, although McCarthy found reversals at some ages. In the present study the percentage is 1.1 for 5½-year-old boys, but only 0.3 for girls of 5½, and it approches the zero point at the later ages. A shift of emphasis, however, might have placed many instances of imaginative play in which toys were personified under this category instead of under that of description.

TABLE 36. — MEAN PERCENTAGES OF TOTAL REMARKS WHICH WERE EGOCENTRIC, AS FOUND BY MCCARTHY (80) AND BY DAVIS

Age in Years	Boys	Girls	Both Sexes
	McCarthy		
4	1.6	1.1	1.3
4½	1.8	2.7	2.2
	Davis		
5½	0.5	0.2	0.4
6½	0.3	0.2	0.2
9½	0.9	0.6	0.7

Incomplete remarks and other minor categories. — At 5½ years 1.24 per cent of all remarks were too fragmentary or too poorly enunciated for classification under the functional categories. Among the older children the percentage drops to .32.

In several of the minor categories the data afford a suggestion that the examiner's impression of a sex difference may be correct, although the total incidence of the type of remark under consideration is too small for statistical verification. Thus quantitative discrimination and ownership were more frequent in boys, and comparisons were more often made by girls. Twins mentioned ownership a little more frequently than singletons and only children. These and similar small differences may be of importance in subsequent research.

Distribution of single-word expressions among the functional categories. — Although the single-word utterances recorded in this situation are functionally very different from the single-word sentences which play so important a part in the language development of young children, they are sufficiently numerous and diversified to repay analysis. Table 37 shows that at all ages and for both sexes

TABLE 37. — DISTRIBUTION OF SINGLE-WORD EXPRESSIONS AMONG THE SEVERAL FUNCTIONAL CATEGORIES

CATEGORY	5½-Year Group			6½-Year Group			9½-Year Group			TOTAL		
	Boys	Girls	Both	Boys	Girls	Both	Boys	Girls	Both	Boys	Girls	Both
Naming	131	179	310	32	17	49	63	5	68	226	201	427
Quantitative discrimination .	3	2	5	0	1	1	0	0	0	3	3	6
Ownership	0	1	1	0	0	0	0	0	0	0	1	1
Comparison	1	0	1	0	0	0	0	1	1	1	1	2
Classification	11	2	13	2	2	4	0	0	0	13	4	17
Judgment	28	31	59	7	7	14	13	10	23	48	48	96
Definition	0	0	0	0	0	0	0	0	0	0	0	0
Description.	11	8	19	0	3	3	4	1	6	15	12	27
Associated with situation .	1	2	3	0	0	0	0	1	2	1	4	5
Associated with conversation .	144	128	272	30	28	58	85	108	193	259	264	523
Irrelevant	0	0	0	0	0	0	0	0	0	0	0	0
Emotionally toned	155	203	358	36	33	69	35	64	99	226	300	526
Questions	99	102	201	25	15	40	8	8	16	132	125	257
Answers	560	674	1234	167	133	300	216	320	536	943	1127	2070
Social phrases.	0	1	1	0	0	0	0	1	1	0	2	2
Dramatic imitation	40	8	48	4	0	4	0	0	0	44	8	52
Egocentric remarks	14	6	20	2	1	3	0	0	0	16	7	23
Incomplete remarks	30	25	55	1	2	3	5	4	9	36	31	67
Total	1228	1372	2600	306	242	548	429	524	953	1963	2138	4101

the vast majority of these single-word utterances are answers — rather a humiliating discovery in view of the fact that, following the procedure of Day and McCarthy, the author tried throughout the study to avoid making remarks to the children which could be answered by an unqualified "yes" or "no." It is true that the category of answers is uniformly the largest, but whereas only 24

TABLE 38. — CORRELATION BETWEEN RANK ORDER OF FUNCTIONAL CATEGORIES WHEN SINGLE-WORD EXPRESSIONS AND OTHER REMARKS ARE BASIS OF RANKING

Group	ρ	PE
5½ years.	.67	.09
6½ years.	.51	.12
9½ years.	.57	.11
Boys	.65	.09
Girls	.63	.10
All	.63	.10

per cent of all remarks are answers, 50 per cent of the single-word remarks fall into this category. For the group as a whole, for all the girls, and for the 5½- and 6½-year groups, the next most important category in number of single-word remarks is emotionally toned remarks, which when all responses are considered falls to ninth place for girls and tenth for boys. Third in rank are remarks

TABLE 39. — CORRELATION BETWEEN AGE AND SEX GROUPS IN RANK ORDER OF FUNCTIONAL CATEGORIES

Groups Compared	Single Word		All Responses	
	ρ	PE	ρ	PE
5½ and 6½ years	.97	.01	.96	.01
5½ and 9½ years	.85	.05	.91	.03
Boys and girls	.97	.01	.95	.02

associated with conversation (sometimes only arbitrarily distinguished from answers, as pointed out above), which hold seventh place when all remarks are considered. Questions rank fifth among single-word expressions, and fourth among all remarks.

If now we rank all the single-word expressions according to functional categories and correlate them by the rank-differences method with a similar ranking of all responses, we find an appreciable relationship. This is given in Table 38. A very high correlation between the rankings of functional categories exists for age and sex groups, but the relationship is no greater when only single-word expressions are considered than when all remarks are taken into account. (See Table 39.) We may conclude that among the single-word remarks, answers, emotionally toned remarks, and remarks associated with conversation are the important categories. A uniform pattern for all age and sex groups may be detected, but although it differs slightly from that found among the remarks as a whole, it is not more consistent. Of the 257 single-word questions, 118 were modifications of the commonly used "hunh" or "hm." "What" occurred 41 times, "where" 12 times, "why" and "who" 8 times each, and "how" 6 times. The remainder were for the most part such expressions as "this," "here," "me," and the like.

Summary

1. Answers constitute the most important category at all ages. They are more frequent at 9½ than at 5½ years.

2. Boys make more spontaneous remarks than girls.

3. Children from the upper occupational groups make more spontaneous remarks than children from the lower occupational groups, but the difference decreases with age.

4. The percentage of answers is highest for singletons and lowest for only children. At 5½ and 6½ years the difference between twin, singleton, and only boys is very slight, but only girls make very few answers in comparison with twin and singleton girls. At 9½ years a high percentage of answers is characteristic of all girls, but the percentage is low for twin and only boys.

5. The percentage of questions decreases with age. Boys ask more questions than girls at each age. At 5½ and 6½ years children from the upper occupational groups ask more questions than children from the lower occupational groups. There is a suggestion that only children ask more questions than other children.

6. Judgment is a category second in importance to answers, but analysis reveals no consistent group differences.

7. Emotionally toned remarks decrease with age and are most common in girls and in only children.

8. Approximately 70 per cent of emotionally toned remarks and 40 per cent of answers are one word in length.

9. In general, single-word expressions are distributed throughout the functional categories in much the same order as other remarks.

VI. COMPLEXITY AND ACCURACY OF SENTENCE STRUCTURE

Phases of Construction Studied

Several aspects of sentence structure were considered in studying the grammatical composition of the language records. First, all the remarks were classified according to an expansion of McCarthy's method. Next, all remarks containing subordinate clauses were analyzed to determine the frequency of the various types of clauses and to obtain the ratio of dependent predicates to the total number of predicates for comparison with the findings of LaBrant (69). Although her ratio has not yet been verified by other investigators for written material, it seemed well worth while to determine the ratio for spoken material. Very little quantitative work has been done with grammatical errors, while the extent and function of use of the auxiliary verb in the language of growing children have hardly been mentioned in the literature. Both these analyses have been made.

OUTLINE OF CLASSIFICATION USED IN CONSTRUCTION ANALYSIS (AFTER MCCARTHY)

I. Complete sentences
   A. Functionally complete but structurally incomplete. This includes naming, answers in which omitted words are implied because they were expressed in the question, expletives, and other remarks, incomplete in themselves, which are clearly a continuation of the preceding remark.
   B. Simple sentence without phrase
   C. Simple sentence containing
      1. Phrase used as adjective or adverb or in apposition
      2. Compound subject or object
      3. Compound predicate
   D. Complex sentence (one main clause, one subordinate clause)
      1. Noun clause, used as
         a. Subject
         b. Object
         c. In apposition
         d. As predicate nominative

   e. As objective complement
  2. Adjective clause
   a. Restrictive
   b. Nonrestrictive
  3. Adverbial clause of time, place, manner, comparison, condition, concession, cause, purpose, and result
  4. Infinitive
 E. Compound sentence (two independent clauses)
 F. Elaborated sentence
  1. Simple sentence with two or more phrases, or compound subject or predicate and phrase
  2. Complex sentence with more than one subordinate clause, or with a phrase or phrases
  3. Compound sentence with more than two independent clauses, or with a subordinate clause or phrases

II. Incomplete sentences

 A. Fragmentary or incomprehensible. Example: "Well — not this, but —."
 B. Verb omitted
  1. Completely
  2. Auxiliary omitted, verb or participle expressed
  3. Verb or participle omitted, auxiliary expressed
 C. Subject omitted, either from main or subordinate clause
 D. Introductory "there" omitted
 E. Pronoun other than subject of verb omitted
 F. Preposition (usually needed sign of infinitive) omitted
 G. Verb and subject omitted
 H. Main clause incomplete, subordinate clause or second clause of compound sentence complete
 I. Main clause complete, subordinate or second clause incomplete. Example: "I know why."
 J. Omissions from both main and subordinate clauses
 K. Essential words present, but sentence loosely constructed because of
  1. Omission of conjunction
  2. Insertion of parenthetical clause
  3. Changes in form halfway in sentence. Example: "We have — my brother has a motorcycle."
 L. Article omitted
  1. Definite
  2. Indefinite
 M. Object omitted either from main clause or prepositional phrase
 N. Sentence left dangling

PROCEDURE

It was necessary to go through the data three times. First the remarks were classified according to the above outline, the author at the same time noting grammatical errors and listing the frequencies of the different verbs used as auxiliaries. Next the subordinate clauses were listed. This required a review of all the data because many remarks containing complete subordinate clauses were classified as functionally complete, or main clause incomplete, or oftenest of all as elaborated sentences. Finally, the number of independent predicates used by each child was listed, for purposes of subordination index, and the occurrence of errors and of auxiliary verbs was checked.

FINDINGS

The construction analysis according to the above outline revealed no consistent differences between twins, singletons, and only children at the three age levels represented. The percentage of functionally complete but structurally incomplete remarks at all ages and for all groups is less than that recorded for Day's (31) 4½- and 5-year-old twins, but it is comparable to that given by McCarthy (80) for her 4½-year-old singletons. The percentage of incomplete sentences, however, while comparable to Day's findings, is at all ages markedly greater than that found by McCarthy, and the percentage of this type of remark increases with age. In fact, it is greater for all groups than that reported by either Day or McCarthy at 4½ years. This may be due to the situation under which the records were obtained; on the other hand, it is possible that the same thing would be found in the language of adults recorded under similar circumstances. These incomplete remarks have not been considered according to the fourteen subheads under which they were classified, but have all been thrown into one group. The percentage of elaborated sentences is appreciably greater at the successive age levels, while the simple sentences without a phrase measurably decrease. The comparison with the Day and McCarthy findings is made in Table 40.

Sex differences are very slight, but when upper and lower occupational groups are compared there appears to be a definite trend in the lower group toward more functionally complete remarks and in the upper group toward more complex and elaborated remarks. The incomplete remarks are not consistently more common in children from the lower occupational group, although there is a difference of 7.4 points in 9½-year-old girls. At 5½ years, however, the difference is in the opposite direction. Sex and occupational differences are shown in Table 41. These findings are in keeping with those of Day and McCarthy.

In the language of preschool children the decrease with age in percentage of incomplete responses is very consistent for all the studies reported. Nice's (93) monthly record of one girl shows a

TABLE 40. — MEAN PERCENTAGES OF TOTAL REMARKS FALLING WITHIN EACH CONSTRUCTIONAL CATEGORY, AS FOUND BY DAY (31),* McCARTHY (80),† AND DAVIS

Type of Sentence	Age in Years	Investigator	Twins	Singletons	Only Children
Functionally complete but structurally incomplete	4½	Day, McCarthy	47	31.2	
	5	Day	49		
	5½	Davis	38.0	39.4	36.4
	6½		28.6	32.0	29.8
	9½		34.8	33.6	33.6
Simple without phrase	4½	Day, McCarthy	28	36.5	
	5	Day	24		
	5½	Davis	31.4	29.4	30.4
	6½		32.2	30.8	31.2
	9½		22.2	18.8	19.8
Simple with phrase	4½	Day, McCarthy	8	10.4	
	5	Day	7		
	5½	Davis	7.8	7.8	8.2
	6½		10.8	9.8	9.8
	9½		10.8	11.4	11.2
Compound and complex	4½	Day, McCarthy	1.6	7.0	
	5	Day	3.6		
	5½	Davis	4.6	4.6	4.8
	6½		7.4	5.4	6.8
	9½		5.4	6.8	6.0
Elaborated	4½	Day, McCarthy	0.9	5.9	
	5	Day	1.0		
	5½	Davis	2.8	3.6	3.8
	6½		5.8	5.6	6.2
	9½		10.2	10.0	11.2
Incomplete	4½	Day, McCarthy	14.5	8.8	
	5	Day	15.4		
	5½	Davis	15.4	15.0	16.4
	6½		15.2	16.4	16.2
	9½		16.6	19.4	18.2

* Twins.   † Singletons.

decrease from 100 per cent incomplete at 21 months to 10 per cent at 43 months; Fisher (36) reported a decrease with age; and Smith (122) reports 37 per cent complete sentences at two years but 87 per cent complete at five years. More records of informal conversation by children of the ages included in the present study should be obtained.

Use of Subordinate Clauses

PREVIOUS INVESTIGATIONS

Complex sentences are so infrequent in preschool children that few analyses have been attempted. Nice (94) reports only one or two complex and compound sentences in each fifty sentences, while McCarthy (80) found that the number remains small throughout the preschool period, although it increases in her older groups. Her

TABLE 41. — MEAN PERCENTAGES OF TOTAL REMARKS MADE BY CHILDREN FROM UPPER AND LOWER OCCUPATIONAL GROUPS WHICH FELL WITHIN EACH CONSTRUCTIONAL CATEGORY

TYPE OF SENTENCE	Occu- pational Group	5½-Year Group			6½-Year Group			9½-Year Group		
		Boys	Girls	Both	Boys	Girls	Both	Boys	Girls	Both
Functionally complete but structurally incomplete	Upper	35.2	33.4	34.2	29.6	27.2	28.4	27.6	36.2	32.0
	Lower	36.6	44.2	40.4	33.8	28.2	31.2	38.0	32.6	35.2
	Both	36.0	39.0	37.4	31.8	27.8	29.8	32.6	34.2	33.6
Simple without phrase	Upper	31.6	31.0	31.4	31.4	31.4	31.4	19.2	20.8	20.0
	Lower	31.8	27.4	29.6	31.2	31.0	31.0	18.8	20.4	19.6
	Both	31.8	29.2	30.4	31.2	31.2	31.2	19.0	20.6	19.8
Simple with phrase	Upper	8.4	8.4	8.4	9.0	8.8	9.0	12.0	12.2	12.2
	Lower	8.8	7.2	8.0	10.6	11.0	10.8	8.2	12.2	10.2
	Both	8.6	7.8	8.2	9.8	9.8	9.8	10.2	12.2	11.2
Compound and complex	Upper	5.4	5.0	5.2	6.4	10.0	8.2	8.2	5.2	6.8
	Lower	4.2	4.4	4.4	5.4	6.0	5.6	4.4	7.0	5.6
	Both	4.8	4.6	4.8	5.8	8.0	6.8	6.2	6.0	6.0
Elaborated	Upper	3.2	5.0	4.2	6.6	6.8	6.6	12.6	14.6	13.6
	Lower	3.2	3.4	3.4	5.6	5.8	5.6	9.2	9.4	9.2
	Both	3.2	4.2	3.8	6.0	6.4	6.2	10.8	11.8	11.2
Incomplete	Upper	16.2	17.2	16.6	17.0	15.8	16.4	21.4	11.0	15.4
	Lower	15.4	13.4	14.2	13.4	18.0	15.8	21.4	18.4	20.2
	Both	15.6	15.2	15.4	15.4	16.8	16.2	21.4	15.2	18.2

category of elaborated sentences contains many subordinate clauses, and the percentage for this type of remark increases markedly with age. She detected no noticeable sex difference in number of complex sentences, but the elaborated sentence appeared earlier in girls and was more frequent. Day (31) found twins decidedly inferior to singletons in both complex and elaborated sentences. Stalnaker's (129) percentages were 2.44 complex and 1.4 compound.

Jespersen (60) believed that men are more inclined to subordination and women to coordination. Piaget (102), Isaacs (59), and Katz (65) have listed many remarks and conversations of young children in illustration of their own theories concerning the development of the reasoning process, but have undertaken no quantitative analysis. Woodcock (160) searched a great mass of monthly full-day language records, besides much language material incidental to other observations, for the first appearance in the child's speech of "why," "because," "so that," and "if." Although she did not treat her material statistically, her findings are probably valid, for they confirm the impressions of other workers and accord with our knowledge of the importance of these words in the vocabulary. The expressions studied appeared almost simultaneously, although "if" tended to lag a little. The beginning of causal thinking, she believes, is obscured by the use of "pre-forms" such as "and" instead of "so that," or by the omission of the conjunction entirely, but the causal relationship may be detected by inserting a "why" between two successive clauses. (Both the use of pre-forms and the omission of the conjunction were frequent in the data analyzed for the present study.) Guillaume (48) points out the necessity of considering pauses and enunciation in deciding what constitutes a child's sentence, and Bloch (12) traces the gradual process by which ideas become subordinate, "even in the absence of the term of subordination." During the third year all three of his children made frequent use of clauses of cause, time, purpose, and condition, but they always began by simple juxtaposition, and even after they learned the conjunctions they often omitted them. Boyd's (17) daughter at the age of three was using 14 subordinate clauses per hundred principal clauses and at seven years her ratio of 30 subordinate clauses was not far below the ratio of 37 which he found for his men and women novelists.

O'Shea (99) tried to determine the order of appearance of conjunctions in his own children but obtained no definite evidence. He was convinced that "none of the conjunctions expressing refined shades of meaning is employed with precision before the fifth year." V at 6½ did not use any of them correctly, but H at 9 used them all fluently. He believed that their use by young children is due to example rather than to the necessity of expressing such complex ideas.

Stormzand (135) analyzed ten thousand sentences selected from essays, newspaper articles and editorials, modern light fiction, adult letters, and compositions of university, high school, and fourth- to eighth-grade students, to determine the actual use of various grammatical forms stressed in teaching. Since only one thousand sentences were taken from the fourth- to eighth-grade children, and we do not know that these were taken in order of occurrence, direct comparisons with the findings of the present study are not entirely satisfactory. Findings are stated in terms of ratios and percentages, however, and since for certain phases of language usage these are the only quantitative expressions extant in the literature, comparison with them was preferable to no comparisons at all. The reader is asked to keep in mind in all subsequent discussions the fact that the Stormzand determinations were made on written material from a small sampling of fourth-grade children and that the basis of selection for both the material and the subjects is unknown.

LaBrant (69) has recently attempted to measure progress in language development by computing the ratio of subordinate clauses to the total number of predicates. She used written material from 482 fourth- to eighth-grade pupils, 504 ninth- to twelfth-grade pupils, and 21 psychologists, a total of 20,320 predicates obtained from 161,518 words. The subordination index was computed for each child and mean and median indexes were obtained for each ten months of mental age between 101 and 230 months and each ten months of chronological age between 101 and 190 months. The mean index for Group A (grade school pupils) was 28.0; for Group B (high school pupils), 36.15; and for the psychologists in Group C, 45.9. The mean index increased steadily with both mental and chronological age, and coefficients of correlation by the Pearsonian product-moment method showed a positive relationship of .29 between subordination index and mental age and .41 between subordination index and chronological age. There was no sex difference.

Anderson (2) obtained 150-word samples from four compositions of a group of college students. The intercorrelations between the four samples for the subordination index were very low and suggest that 150 words is entirely too short a sample to yield a stable index.

Number of subordinate clauses. — The mean number of subordinate clauses increases with age and is somewhat greater for girls

TABLE 42. — MEAN NUMBER OF SUBORDINATE CLAUSES USED BY CHILDREN FROM UPPER AND LOWER OCCUPATIONAL GROUPS

GROUPS	TWINS		SINGLETONS		ONLY CHILDREN		ALL		
	Boys	Girls	Boys	Girls	Boys	Girls	Boys	Girls	Both
5½ years									
Upper occupational	3.3	4.2	4.4	5.1	6.1	8.1	4.4	5.4	4.9
Lower occupational	3.3	3.6	3.5	2.7	4.1	6.9	3.4	3.9	3.7
Both	3.3	3.9	3.9	3.8	5.1	7.5	3.9	4.6	4.3
6½ years									
Upper occupational	7.6	11.6	4.0	5.8	8.2	8.0	6.6	8.3	7.5
Lower occupational	3.2	2.5	4.8	4.0	4.6	6.2	4.2	4.0	4.2
Both	5.2	6.6	4.4	5.0	6.4	7.2	5.3	6.2	5.8
9½ years									
Upper occupational	12.4	10.3	10.3	7.8	13.0	8.2	11.7	8.9	10.3
Lower occupational	4.0	3.7	7.2	10.7	15.2	12.1	7.5	8.4	8.0
Both	8.2	7.0	8.6	9.4	14.1	10.3	9.5	8.7	9.1

than for boys, for children from the upper occupational groups than for children from the lower occupational groups, and for only children than for twins and for singletons with siblings. These differences are shown in Table 42.

TABLE 43. — MEAN NUMBER OF SUBORDINATE CLAUSES USED PER HUNDRED SENTENCES

AGE IN YEARS	TWINS		SINGLETONS		ONLY CHILDREN	
	Boys	Girls	Boys	Girls	Boys	Girls
5½	6.7	7.8	7.8	7.7	10.1	15.1
6½	10.4	13.3	8.9	10.0	12.8	14.4
9½	16.4	14.0	17.3	18.8	28.2	20.6

In the Stormzand study (135) the number of dependent clauses per hundred sentences ranged from 24 for fourth-grade compositions to 143 for Stevenson, with the adult average at 97. The ratio of dependent clauses to each hundred sentences is easily computed from Table 43, which shows 8, 11, and 18 dependent clauses used per hundred sentences at the successive age levels. For the 9½-year-old only children the percentage ratio is exactly 24, the figure reported by Stormzand for the fourth-grade children. Table 43 gives the distribution of the percentage ratios.

TABLE 44. — MEAN NUMBER OF SUBORDINATE CLAUSES USED
PER THOUSAND WORDS

Age in Years	Boys	Girls	Both Sexes
5½	17	20	19
6½	21	23	22
9½	30	26	28

TABLE 45. —MEAN NUMBER OF SUBORDINATE CLAUSES USED
PER THOUSAND WORDS BY ONLY CHILDREN

Age in Years	Boys	Girls	Both Sexes
5½	22	27	24
6½	25	25	25
9½	38	28	33

Since the distribution of subordinate clauses so nearly parallels the distribution according to sentence length, it is possible that the apparent group differences in number of subordinate clauses result from variations in sentence length. The probability of a real difference appears, however, when the mean number of subordinate clauses is related to each thousand words used, as is done in Table 44.

In the same way Table 45 shows that only children are at each age well above the mean in the ratio of subordinate clauses to total words used.

Similar differences would seem probable when the number of subordinate clauses is related to the total number of predicates, as was done in LaBrant's study (69). In adapting LaBrant's procedure to spoken material some difficulties were encountered. The criterion for a complete predicate is much less clear cut than in written language, because very often the main clause is understood or cryptically expressed, while the subordinate clause is complete. This is especially true in answers. For example:

E. Why did they use oxen to pull the wagons instead of horses?
S. Because they didn't have horses in those old times.

Again, in many sentences the second clause is probably subordinate in the child's thought, but the relationship is not expressed. Thus in the sentence, "There's a little girl, she goes upstairs over me," the function of the second clause is undoubtedly that of a restrictive adjective, but the sentence was classified as containing two independent clauses, incomplete because of the omitted conjunction. Many such instances verify Woodcock's conclusions (160). Furthermore, the spoken records contain large numbers of one-word and

TABLE 46. — RELATION BETWEEN NUMBER OF SUBORDINATE CLAUSES
AND TOTAL NUMBER OF PREDICATES
(In percentages of number of predicates)

GROUP	TWINS		SINGLETONS		ONLY CHILDREN		ALL		
	Boys	Girls	Boys	Girls	Boys	Girls	Boys	Girls	Both
5½ years									
Upper occupational . .	8	9	11	11	13	16	10	12	11
Lower occupational . .	8	9	8	8	10	14	9	9	9
Both	8	9	9	9	12	15	9	11	10
6½ years									
Upper occupational . .	15	22	9	12	16	13	13	16	15
Lower occupational . .	7	6	12	8	11	12	10	8	9
Both	11	14	10	10	14	13	12	12	12
9½ years									
Upper occupational . .	20	19	20	15	24	16	21	17	19
Lower occupational . .	9	9	16	18	21	20	15	16	16
Both	16	15	18	17	22	18	18	16	17

fragmentary remarks that would not be found even in the most immature written language. For all these reasons one would expect the index of subordination even for the 9½-year group to be well below that of LaBrant's Group A. This was found to be the case, but Table 46 shows that the index increases slightly with age and is a little higher for only children and for children from the upper occupational classes. No consistent sex difference appears.

Types of subordinate clauses. — The relative importance of noun, adjectival, and adverbial clauses seems to vary somewhat with age, but perhaps even more with the type of material analyzed. The percentages reported by various investigators are summarized in Table 47.

TABLE 47. — PERCENTAGES OF EACH TYPE OF SUBORDINATE CLAUSE USED AT DIFFERENT LEVELS, AS FOUND BY SEVERAL INVESTIGATORS

Investigator	Subjects	Noun Clause	Adjectival Clause	Adverbial Clause
Stormzand (135)	4th grade children	38.9	22.1	38.9
	Adults *	31.2	32.1	36.7
Boyd (17)	Child in 3d year	34	20	47
	Child in 9th year	42	13	46
	Men novelists	42	16	42
	Women novelists	41	13	46
LaBrant (69)	Grade school pupils	23.8	21.4	54.7
Davis	Children aged 5½	48.3	23.3	28.3
	Children aged 6½	48.2	20.1	31.2
	Children aged 9½	31.5	16.5	52.0

* Average for Stormzand's own subjects and excerpts from literature and letters.

For the age groups considered in the present study it appears that adjectival clauses are the least important, that the number of noun clauses decreases during the early school years, and that the number of adverbial clauses increases. It is possible that increased precision in the use of language accounts for these changes in percentage, rather than a true functional variation. Thus, as will be shown below, adverbial clauses of place are infrequent, while those of time are common. But, as LaBrant noted, many place clauses are so expressed as to necessitate classification as adjectival. LaBrant found that the percentage of adjectival clauses doubles between

TABLE 48. — PERCENTAGES OF EACH TYPE OF SUBORDINATE CLAUSE USED BY CHILDREN FROM UPPER AND LOWER OCCUPATIONAL GROUPS

Group	Noun		Adjectival		Adverbial	
	Boys	Girls	Boys	Girls	Boys	Girls
5½ years						
Upper occupational	53.5	47.5	23.4	21.6	23.4	30.9
Lower occupational	45.5	46.7	31.1	17.1	23.4	36.1
Both	49.7	47.1	27.0	19.6	23.4	33.2
6½ years						
Upper occupational	38.4	55.6	25.2	16.5	36.4	27.8
Lower occupational	47.9	51.7	25.3	13.3	26.8	35.0
Both	42.3	54.4	25.3	15.5	32.3	30.0
9½ years						
Upper occupational	35.9	19.1	16.2	16.5	47.9	64.4
Lower occupational	29.6	39.4	17.1	16.5	53.5	44.1
Both	33.3	29.5	16.6	16.5	50.1	54.0

the mental ages of 101 and 230 months. Table 48, which gives the percentage of each type of clause according to age and occupational groups, shows no consistent differences.

The three types of subordinate clauses may be further classified according to their function. In the spoken material four uses of noun clauses were distinguished. The vast majority were used by all groups as the object of a verb, or occasionally of a preposition. The predicate nominative was second in importance, with an occasional appositive clause. There were only three examples of a noun clause used as the subject of a verb. The uses of noun clauses are summarized in Table 49.

TABLE 49. — PERCENTAGE DISTRIBUTION OF DIFFERENT TYPES OF NOUN CLAUSES, AS FOUND BY STORMZAND (135) AND BY DAVIS

Investigator	Group	Object of Verb or Preposition	Predicate Nominative	Apposition	Subject	Others
Davis	5½ years	80.1	15.5	3.8	0.5	0.0
	6½ years	85.2	14.3	0.5	0.0	0.0
	9½ years	89.2	8.1	2.6	0.0	0.0
Stormzand (135)	4th grade	95.8	4.4	0.0	0.0	0.0
	Children and adults *	74.4	5.1	18.2	1.6	0.7

* Average for Stormzand's own subjects and excerpts from literature and letters.

Because of the relative unimportance of adjectival clauses they were not classified for restrictive and nonrestrictive function, but most of them were of the restrictive type. Adverbial clauses fell into eight groups. The categories of purpose and result, which LaBrant could not differentiate, offered no difficulty, but there was so much confusion between manner and comparison that the two categories were finally thrown together. LaBrant found clauses of condition, concession, place, purpose, result, and comparison of negligible importance, amounting only to about 6 per cent of the total clauses. In the present study, however, the total percentage for these types of clauses is 17.7, with 453 of the 2,564 subordinate clauses falling into these categories. The distribution of the adverbial clauses is given in Table 50.

Among sentences of Stormzand's fourth graders 52 per cent of the adverbial clauses were time clauses, 26 per cent condition, 13.1 per cent cause and evidence, and 4.4 per cent clauses of manner and comparison. These categories, therefore, included 95.6 per cent of all adverbial clauses at this level.

LaBrant, Stormzand, and Boyd (17) agree with the findings of the present study as to the primary importance of time clauses, which make up roughly 20 to 50 per cent of all the adverbial clauses used by child and adult subjects in both spoken and written material. Boyd does not give exact percentages, but says that nearly all the adverbial clauses found in the compositions of 83 elementary

TABLE 50. — PERCENTAGE DISTRIBUTION OF DIFFERENT TYPES
OF ADVERBIAL CLAUSES

Group	Time	Place	Condition	Cause	Manner and Comparison	Purpose	Result	Concession
Boys of 5½ . . .	31.6	4.4	17.5	18.4	7.9	9.6	7.9	3.5
Girls of 5½ . . .	25.6	8.4	9.9	28.8	7.8	8.4	9.4	1.6
Boys of 6½ . . .	22.6	0.0	18.9	28.3	18.9	5.7	5.7	0.0
Girls of 6½ . . .	21.7	1.7	16.7	28.3	10.0	5.0	15.0	1.7
Boys of 9½ . . .	21.6	2.0	14.9	31.1	8.1	13.5	6.7	2.0
Girls of 9½ . . .	22.4	2.7	10.8	39.3	4.4	10.2	9.1	1.0

school pupils which he analyzed were clauses of time. Clauses of place, on the other hand, are infrequent in all the studies, usually making up only 2 or 3 per cent of the adverbial clauses.

USE OF THE INFINITIVE

Stormzand (135) found the number of nonmodal verb forms per sentence to be 0.7. Of these 56.8 per cent are infinitives, 27.0 per cent are participles, and the remaining 16.2 per cent are gerunds. The number of infinitives per sentence was 0.2 in fourth-grade material and increased to .51 for university upper classmen, with an adult average of .42. LaBrant (69) noted that children frequently employ the infinitive with a form of the verbs "to be" or "to go" to form the future tense, and listed such uses as auxiliary. Her procedure has been adopted in the present study. She listed 1,244 infinitives in her A group, which when related to the 2,507 subordinate predicates gave a ratio of 2.05 to 1.

For the spoken material the number of infinitives increases somewhat with age, although the rate of increase is somewhat lessened when the number is related to sentence length. The mean number of infinitives for boys and girls at each age is given in Table 51. At 5½ years the number of infinitives per sentence was .03, at 6½ years .04, and at 9½ years .10. The same trend is shown when the ratio of subordinate clauses to infinitives is computed; that is, there are fewer subordinate predicates to each infinitive at 9½ than at

TABLE 51. — MEAN NUMBER OF INFINITIVES USED

Age in Years	Boys	Girls	Both Sexes
5½	1.4	1.7	1.6
6½	1.8	2.3	2.0
9½	4.3	5.3	4.8

TABLE 52. — RATIO OF NUMBER OF SUBORDINATE CLAUSES TO NUMBER OF INFINITIVES USED

Age in Years	Boys	Girls	Both Sexes
5½	2.70	2.79	2.75
6½	2.98	2.68	2.81
9½	2.21	1.63	1.89

5½ years, which is contrary to the findings of LaBrant. The ratios by age and sex are given in Table 52. Only children consistently use more infinitives than twins and singletons with siblings. This is also true when the number of infinitives is related to sentence length, but there is no consistent difference in the ratio of subordinate clauses to number of infinitives.

USE OF AUXILIARY VERBS

The English language depends very largely upon the common auxiliary verbs for the expression of voice, mood and interrogation, negation, emphatic and progressive tense forms, and the formation of future and compound tenses. Since practically all these auxiliary verbs are irregularly conjugated, and since Stormzand (135) assures us that they are used three times as often as all other irregular verbs put together, it is rather surprising that their use by young children has not been studied.

School grammars usually list the auxiliary verbs as "be" in all its forms, "have," "has," "had," "shall," "will," "may," "can," "must," "might," "could," "would," "should," "do," "did," and "ought." Since many texts add the words, "and the like," the disposition of a given construction is left to individual preference. The most frequent example in spoken language is the use of "going" to express futurity or intention. The writer has found no text which mentions this verb as an auxiliary, yet when a child says, "I am going to put these here," he is of course not going anywhere, but means "I shall put these here." The disposition of this expression is of considerable importance, because in the present study it occurred 738 times. LaBrant (69) classified this use of "go" as auxiliary, and the same procedure was followed in the present study. The next most difficult decision had to do with the word "got," an elastic and much overworked verb form which is becoming recognized in spoken English in spite of the authorities. The rules followed were these:

1. "I've got one of these at home." "Got" disregarded, since it is used only to add emphasis to "have," the main verb.

2. "I have got to go." "Have" listed as auxiliary in the sense of "must"; "got" disregarded as an intensive.

3. "I got to go." "Got" listed as auxiliary, in the sense of "must."

4. "He got hurt." "Got" listed as auxiliary, to form the passive voice.

Our list of auxiliary verbs could be greatly extended by following the analogy of other languages. Thus in German many verbs expressing shades of meaning are considered auxiliary, as *lassen, dürfen, wissen*; the subjunctive expresses doubt or uncertainty; and the causative and periphrastic auxiliaries have a definite place. Conversely, Greek and Latin by suffixes and modifications in the verb stem can express very complicated variations in mood and tense without recourse to auxiliary verbs. Although it was a temptation to experiment with verbs of trying, wishing, and needing, the list was finally limited to the following:

"Be" in all its forms, as passive, progressive, etc.

"Do," "did," without distinguishing emphatic, negative, and interrogative functions

"Can," "could" meaning either ability or permission

"Will," "would"

"Go" expressing futurity or intention

"Have" used in forming perfect tenses

"Have" in the sense of "must"

"Have" as a causative: "I had him go back"

"Shall," "should"
"May," "might"
"Must"
"Ought"
"Got" in the sense of "must"
"Got" as passive
"Had" better or "had" rather
"Used" in the sense of "was accustomed"
"Get to" or "got to": "He gets to go next"
"Keep" in the sense of "continue"

When the tabulation was completed, it was found that the first six verbs comprised 95 per cent of all the auxiliaries, and the last

TABLE 53. — MEAN OCCURRENCE OF MOST COMMON AUXILIARY VERBS IN CHILDREN FROM UPPER AND LOWER OCCUPATIONAL GROUPS

Group	Be	Do	Can	Will	Go	Have	All Others	Total	Average per 1000 Words
5½ years									
Upper occupational . . .	5.0	2.8	2.0	1.6	1.5	0.7	0.5	14.1	59
Lower occupational . . .	4.6	2.2	1.3	1.2	1.6	0.7	0.4	12.0	55
Both	4.8	2.4	1.7	1.4	1.5	0.7	0.5	13.0	57
6½ years									
Upper occupational . . .	4.2	3.4	2.0	3.2	1.5	1.2	1.1	16.6	59
Lower occupational . . .	6.1	2.1	1.2	1.7	1.5	0.6	0.8	14.0	56
Both	5.2	2.7	1.6	2.4	1.5	0.9	1.0	15.3	58
9½ years									
Upper occupational . . .	9.4	2.0	2.5	3.8	2.3	1.6	1.2	22.8	66
Lower occupational . . .	8.5	1.8	3.0	3.5	2.0	1.1	1.3	21.2	68
Both	9.0	1.9	2.8	3.6	2.1	1.3	1.3	22.0	67

three were so infrequent that their omission or inclusion was immaterial. The mean occurrence of each of the six most common auxiliaries in the upper and lower occupational groups at each of the three age levels is given in Table 53, together with the total number of uses of all forms by each group and the average number per thousand words used by each group. There is very little difference between the upper and lower occupational groups in the total number of auxiliaries used, and practically none when the total number is related to the length of sentence, but there is a slight gain with age. Differences between twins, singletons, and only children were negligible when related to length of sentence.

At all ages there is a very slight difference in favor of girls in the average number of auxiliary verbs per thousand words. (See Table 54.)

The verb "to be" is the most frequently used auxiliary at all ages. It is nearly twice as frequent at 9½ as at 5½ years, and the difference persists, although it is smaller, when the frequency is related to sentence length. It occurs 21 times per thousand words at 5½, 19 times at 6½, and 27 times at 9½ years. A similar increase with age is found in the use of the auxiliary "will." The average use per thousand words is 6 at 5½, 9 at 6½, and 11 at 9½ years.

TABLE 54. — MEAN NUMBER OF AUXILIARY VERBS USED BY DIFFERENT SEX AND SIBLING RELATIONSHIP GROUPS

	BOYS		GIRLS	
GROUP	Mean	Mean per 1000 Words	Mean	Mean per 1000 Words
Twins				
5½ years	12.7	57	12.6	57
6½ years	14.6	53	16.7	63
9½ years	19.9	63	20.4	67
All	15.1	58	15.3	61
Singletons				
5½ years	11.5	52	13.0	59
6½ years	12.6	54	14.1	52
9½ years	19.6	65	25.6	73
All	14.4	58	16.9	64
Only children				
5½ years	14.2	61	15.7	57
6½ years	14.9	59	19.3	66
9½ years	24.2	66	24.0	66
All only children	16.8	62	18.7	62
All groups.	15.2	59	16.7	62

Since both these auxiliaries are largely used in forming complicated verb phrases expressing voice and tense, it seems probable that occurrence would keep pace with the increasing mastery of these forms from year to year.

It is interesting to note how closely O'Shea's (99) observations as to the order of use of the various auxiliaries are borne out by these quantitative findings. "Would," he says, appears before "could," and "should" comes last. "The subtle distinctions giving warrant to and really making necessary the use of 'should' are for the most part beyond the six- or even seven-year-old." The past perfect tense, he states, is never used except mechanically before the eighth or ninth year, and the future perfect not until studied in school. "Will" appears before "shall," which is rare even at ten and eleven years.

Stormzand (135, page 119) gives the relative frequency of the auxiliary verbs for his material. Percentages have been computed

TABLE 55. — PERCENTAGE DISTRIBUTION OF DIF-
FERENT AUXILIARY VERBS, AS FOUND BY
STORMZAND (135) AND BY DAVIS

Verb	Stormzand	Davis
be.	65.9	45.2
shall, will, would, should . . .	12.3	18.4
have (perfect)	10.3	2.6
can, could	4.5	14.8
may, might.	2.4	0.9
must	1.2	0.6
do.	3.1	17.3
ought	0.2	0.1
	99.9	99.9

to make the frequencies comparable to those in the present study. (See Table 55.) The rank orders are identical except for "have" used in forming perfect tenses, which is much more common in the written material, and "do," which is third in importance in the spoken sentences but relatively infrequent in the Stormzand analysis.

GRAMMATICAL ERRORS

There has been very little quantitative study of errors in the speech of young children, although the literature contains many references to characteristic omissions, inflections, and redundancies (12, 13, 17, 48, 60, 66, 88, 99), and some of the theories put forth by the early child biographers are not without merit. Smith (120) analyzed grammatical errors in 99,289 words from the speech of 220 preschool children ranging in age from 18 months to 6 years. She made twelve error classifications, of which one was "omission," and related the total number of errors to the number of words used. This error index was .58 at 2 years, .21 at 3 years, .07 at 4 years, and thereafter remained at .05. There was no sex difference except at 2 years. At 5 and 6 years "the only errors occurring more than once per thousand words are those among the commonest in the speech of adults." All other work with grammatical errors has been done with school children, and consists mainly of tabulations of lists kept by teachers. Several investigators (23, 45, 46, 61, 77, 135) have analyzed grade and high school compositions for errors, and have attempted remedial measures. The main facts discovered by many workers (29, 61, 73, 78, 106, 116, 136, 156, 157, 158) are, first, that a very few common errors make up a large percentage of the total errors; second, that persistent drill has not succeeded in eradicating these from the speech of school children; third, that oral and written errors cannot be judged by the same standard; and fourth, that the method of recording by teachers is far from accurate.

In the present study, the Smith error index was found to hold, with no age, sex, or occupational group differences. Omissions were considered as errors in computing this index, though elsewhere, because one section of the construction analysis was devoted to them, they were not so considered. In presenting group differences, the mean number of errors per thousand words has been employed. This measure indicates that boys make more errors than girls, and children from the lower occupational groups make rather more errors than children from the upper occupational groups. Twin boys make more errors than singleton and only boys, while twin girls exceed only girls in number of errors, but do not exceed singleton girls. The number of errors per thousand words decreases from 32 at 5½ years to 22 at 9½ years. (See Tables 56 and 57.)

By far the most frequent individual error was the use of the verb form "is" instead of "are." The singular verb was used for the plural much oftener than the plural was used for the singular. When all cases of non-agreement between verb and subject were thrown together, the total was 801 instances, or 26 per cent of all errors. The next largest type of error was redundancy, of which there were 479 instances. The most frequent example was the superfluous "here," in such expressions as "this here man." A redundant pronoun form, perhaps intended to emphasize the subject, was very common, in sentences like "This Indian, he comes riding up."

"Got" was considered erroneous only when it was used in place of "have" to denote possession or necessity. Even with the possibility for error thus limited to "I got one of these" and "I got to hurry home tonight," 352 instances were noted; hence this word must be regarded as of considerable importance in the language of growing children.

"A" was used for "an" 155 times, and "ain't" occurred 141 times. The double negative was noted only 75 times, and its inci-

TABLE 56. — MEAN NUMBER OF ERRORS MADE PER THOUSAND WORDS

Group	Boys	Girls	Both Sexes
5½ years			
Upper occupational.	28	29	29
Lower occupational.	39	29	35
Both	34	29	32
6½ years			
Upper occupational.	26	20	23
Lower occupational.	28	23	26
Both	27	21	24
9½ years			
Upper occupational.	23	20	21
Lower occupational.	25	20	23
Both	24	20	22

TABLE 57. — RATIO OF ERRORS TO WORDS IN DIFFERENT AGE
AND SEX GROUPS

Age in Years	Boys	Girls	Both Sexes
5½.	1:29.3	1:33.9	1:31.5
6½.	1:36.6	1:46.3	1:41.0
9½.	1:41.7	1:48.6	1:45.0

dence per thousand words dropped from 0.8 at 5½ years to 0.3 at 9½ years. "Lay" was used instead of "lie" 109 times; and an adjective took the place of an adverb 109 times, the words "awful" and "real" being the ones most often misused in this way. The expressions "kind of" and "sort of" ("I'll put him sort of hiding behind these bushes") were listed 56 times.

Errors of inflection proved of considerable importance. There were 162 instances of difficulty in conjugation of verbs, 130 errors in number, gender, and case of pronouns, and 110 mistakes in the formation of plural nouns, but only 7 errors in the comparison of adjectives. A major cause of these errors of inflection seems to be the tendency noted by Smith (120) to "extend rules for the formation of regular forms to irregular forms." In numerous instances the child attempted to form the preterit of an irregular verb by adding the suffix *ed* ("standed," "sticked," "buyed," "breaked," "teached," "knowed"). In the same way the plural of an irregular or collective noun was formed regularly. In comparing adjectives, the child would say "more bad," "more safer," or "goodest." The largest group of errors in conjugating verbs was the use of the irregular preterit for the participle, which was listed 65 times.

In the use of pronouns the substitution of "them" for "those" was frequent; errors in number and gender were often noted; and

TABLE 58. — SUMMARY OF GRAMMATICAL ERRORS

Error	Frequency	Frequency per 1000 Words	Percentage of All Errors	Charters-Miller Percentage
Verb not in agreement with subject	801	7	26.0	14
Redundancy	479	3	15.5	10
"Got" for "have"	352	3	11.4	..
Errors in conjugation of verbs	162	1	5.2	17
"A" for "an"	155	1	5.0	..
"Ain't"	141	1	4.6	..
Inflection of pronouns	130	1	4.2	..
Plural noun forms	110	1	3.6	..
Wrong preposition or conjunction	114	1	3.7	..
Adjective for adverb	109	0.9	3.5	4
"Lay" for "lie"	109	0.9	3.5	..
Miscellaneous errors in diction	109	0.9	3.5	..
Double negative	75	0.6	2.6	11
Provincialisms and colloquialisms	67	0.6	2.1	..
"Kind of" or "sort of"	56	0.5	1.8	..
Wrong word order	44	0.4	1.4	2
Confused person, number, or tense	36	0.3	1.0	..
Awkward construction	26	0.2	0.8	..
Comparison of adjectives	7	0.1	0.2	..
Total	3082		99.6	

there were several instances of hybrid pronoun forms such as "ourself" or "theirself." There were 36 instances of confusion in person, number, or tense; that is, a part of the subordinate clause failed to agree with its antecedent in one or another of these respects. The wrong preposition or conjunction was used in 114 instances. The outstanding example was the misuse of "like" for "as if," but nearly all the common words in these groups were wrongly used on one or more occasions.

In 44 cases the error consisted of faulty word order, and there were 26 instances of awkward construction, which in turn were sometimes difficult to distinguish from the miscellaneous category of 67 provincialisms, barbarisms, and colloquialisms. Such expressions were "don't guess," "how come?" "anywheres," "youse," "he knows not to," "that's all the pig he's got," and so on.

The relative importance of each group of errors may be estimated by the number of times it occurs per thousand words and its percentage of the total number of errors. Table 58 gives these frequencies, together with comparable percentages from the Charters-Miller Study.

SUMMARY

1. The percentage of remarks which are functionally complete but structurally incomplete decreases slightly with age.

2. Simple sentences without a phrase decrease with age.

3. Simple sentences with a phrase, and compound, complex, and elaborated sentences increase with age.

4. The percentage of incomplete responses is slightly greater at 9½ years than at the earlier ages.

5. There are no consistent differences between twins, singletons, and only children in sentence structure at the ages studied. Sex differences are very slight, but children from the lower occupational groups tend to use more functionally complete but structurally incomplete sentences, while those from the upper groups use more complex and elaborated sentences.

6. The mean number of subordinate clauses increases with age and is greater for children from the upper occupational groups, for only children, and for girls. The difference remains when the number of subordinate clauses is related to the number of words used.

7. The index of subordination (after LaBrant) increases slightly with age, and is a little higher for only children and for children from the upper occupational classes.

8. Adjectival clauses are of least importance at each age level, but while noun clauses are most important at 5½ years, adverbial clauses are most important at 9½ years.

9. Nearly 85 per cent of all noun clauses are used as the object of verbs or occasionally of prepositions.

10. Clauses of cause and of time are the most important adverbial clauses, although in the reports of other investigators based on

written material, clauses of condition are more important than cause.

11. The number of infinitives increases with age, and is slightly greater for girls than for boys. Only children use more infinitives than other children.

12. The use of auxiliary verbs increases slightly with age and is slightly greater for girls than for boys.

13. Forms of the verb "to be" make up about 45 per cent of all auxiliary verbs used. These forms become increasingly important with age.

14. Smith's error index of .05 holds for children at the ages studied.

15. Errors are more common in boys than in girls. The number of errors decreases with age.

VII. FREQUENCY, FUNCTION, AND LENGTH OF THE DIFFERENT WORDS USED

PREVIOUS INVESTIGATIONS

The most widely studied phase of language development has been the size of vocabulary at different ages and its distribution among the parts of speech. Dozens of parents have kept such records for individual children, but with such wide variations in method that no norms could be established. Kirkpatrick's (67) use of the number of words known on a check list selected from the dictionary was at first hailed as a greatly simplified means of measuring vocabulary, but it was soon found that results varied with the dictionary used. Williams (153) maintains that sampling by page units of the dictionary involves a constant error, since words do not occupy a fixed amount of space on a page. He tabulated the words common to a sample of 1,263 words from the *College Standard Dictionary* and the International Kindergarten Union's list of 2,500 children's words. Since the sample comprised 1/111 of the words in the dictionary, there should have been 23 common words; actually the number was 97. Similar results were obtained when the unabridged dictionary and Thorndike's list (140) were used. Williams concludes that the disproportion favors words in common use, with the greatest richness of meaning. Kirkpatrick's (67) study of the parts of speech of words in the dictionary as compared with actual use would indicate that the dictionary method is unreliable for determining the relative percentage of each part of speech in the vocabulary. The vocabulary test, however, remains the "best single test of verbal ability" according to the findings of Schneck (114), who gave five verbal tests to a group of 210 men.

Markey (84) concluded that at 5 years of age the order of frequency with which the several parts of speech are actually used is verbs, pronouns, nouns, adjectives, adverbs. Stalnaker's (129) fourteen children from the upper socio-economic classes used more verbs than other parts of speech. McCarthy's (80) singletons used more nouns than verbs at all ages, whether the percentages were based on total number of words used or number of different words used, but the percentage of verbs was considerably larger in her older than in her younger groups, while the percentage of nouns based on the total number of words decreased markedly. The percentage of nouns based on the number of different words did not change with age. Day's (31) twins used approximately 40 per cent nouns and 22 per cent verbs at each age when the percentages were based on number of different words used, but except for her youngest group the verbs outnumbered the nouns when the total words used were taken as the base. Bloch (13) thinks the early preponderance of nouns may be peculiar to languages such as French, in which nouns are uninflected, and points out the frequent use by young children of a noun meaning action. Zyve's (163) third-grade children used more different nouns than verbs, but the total usage of verbs was much greater. Zipf (162) makes a similar distinction. Smith (125) simplified the usual divisions of parts of speech into five classes, which in their order of importance are substantives, verbs, modifiers, connectives, and interjections.

Numerous lists of words actually used by children have been compiled, usually looking toward revision of spelling courses and preparing primary reading texts or story-telling material. The procedure with children under 6 years is to record conversation in the schoolroom or in an experimental situation, and with older children to tabulate words (6, 27, 64, 101) from compositions or letters. Horn (54) had teachers record conversation of children attending kindergarten. Dolch (33) and Prescott (104) asked their subjects to write down all the words they could think of in fifteen minutes. Dolch obtained from 206 children from the second to the eighth grade 12,622 different words and 2,312,000 running words. Three thousand thirty-nine words were used only once, but all the others were graded for teaching purposes. Prescott, whose subjects were 50 boys and 50 girls at each age between 7 and 13 years, found that the boys wrote down a larger number of different words than the girls. Tidyman (138) classified words under the grades, from the third to the seventh, in which they first appeared. More than a thousand of the three thousand commonest words appeared in the third grade, and the number rapidly decreased from grade to grade thereafter. The Shambaughs (118) by using 400 stimulus words obtained 4,515 different words from 1,851 children distributed through grades 4 to 8, inclusive, and 1,309 of these words were common to all the grades.

Gates (39), Wheeler and Howell (150), and others (112) have compiled lists from primers and similar elementary texts, but the most extensive and systematic work of this nature has been done by Thorndike (140). His original list of ten thousand words published in 1921 was compiled from forty-one sources, notably the Bible and English classics, children's literature, and textbooks, but newspapers, general correspondence, and simple trade texts were represented. Further counts and collaboration with other workers have now extended the list to twenty thousand words with frequencies so indicated that teachers can determine almost at a glance the importance of a word in terms of actual use.

The list compiled by Dewey (32) from periodicals and literature is valuable because it distinguishes particular and root words and also undertakes an analysis of most frequent syllables and sounds. Such lists are primarily of interest to students of linguistic development because of the high percentage of agreement on the most frequent words. Nice (92) points out that the baby's speech is much more individualistic than that of older children, but before the close of the preschool period there is marked agreement in the most common words. Thus six of the sixteen most frequent words used by Stalnaker's (129) fourteen subjects were found on Smith's (122) list of ten most common words. In the standardized vocabulary of 660 words prepared by Hughes for teaching Spanish-speaking children, Sanchez (112) found that 624 are among the commonest words in the spoken vocabulary of children up to 6 years of age as reported by Horn (53). Four hundred six are in the first 500 of the International Kindergarten Union's list (58); 383 in Gates's (39) first 500; 355 in Thorndike's first 500 (140); 526 in Kircher's Primer List; and 380 in the 452 words of Wheeler and Howell (150). Dewey (32) concludes that in a representative sample of connected English, the 10 commonest words will form 25 per cent, the 100 commonest words will form 50 per cent, and the 1,000 commonest words will form 75 per cent.

METHOD OF COMPILING LISTS

Two radically different methods of listing words were considered. It would be feasible to make up a list of common words and check the occurrence of each in the language records, adding supplementary words as they appeared. The second method, which was the one adopted, was to start with an actual record, listing each word in the order of its occurrence. The first sentence recorded for the 9½-year-old only boy from Occupational Group I was, "Shall I set them up in a parade?"; hence the list of words began in this way. New words were added very rapidly at first, but it was soon apparent that the percentage of common words used by subjects in a standardized situation would prove very high. The first two records yielded 204 different words, and throughout the analysis it was found that these original words recurred with astounding frequency. Although no definite computations were made, the percentage was calculated from time to time on completion of an individual record, and the writer is convinced that at least 60 per cent of the words found on all records are distributed among these original 204 words.

As McCarthy (80) has pointed out, there has been little uniformity of procedure among investigators in listing inflected forms, contractions, and different meanings of the same word. The rules laid down by Bateman* and followed by Nice, McCarthy, and others have been adopted with some amplification for the present study. They are summarized below:

1. Proper names, except "Indian," "Christmas," "Santa Claus," "Easter," and "Jesus," were listed in a separate category. When the name was made up of two words, one of which might occur in many combinations, as "Como Park," "Phelps Island," "Buffalo Bill," .the name itself was listed as proper, but the common word was listed in the regular way. The proper adjectives "American," "German," and "French" were listed regularly.

2. Contractions of "not" and an auxiliary verb form were listed individually, but contractions of pronoun and verb were treated as two words.

3. Inflected forms were listed separately when definitely irregular ("man," "men"; "go," "went").

4. "Kinda," "oughta" were counted as two words each, "kind of," "ought to."

5. Faulty inflections were listed under the form which they most closely resembled, regardless of error; thus, "standed" under "stand," not "stood."

6. When the same word was used both as noun and verb it was listed twice ("dance," "park," "guard," "camp," "hunt").

7. Words used with two distinct meanings were listed twice ("like," "back," "well"); but this distinction was not attempted in the case of "have" and "got," nor with adjectives and participles used as substantives, nor adjectives sometimes used as adverbs.

8. Some very common words were not differentiated according to parts of speech. Examples are "this," used both as adjective and pro-

* W. G. Bateman. "Two Children's Progress in Speech," *Journal of Educational Psychology*, 6: 475-93 (1915). Or see McCarthy, *op. cit.*, p. 46.

noun; "that," as adjective, pronoun, and conjunction. In some cases texts disagree in classification, and it seemed better to avoid controversial points which were apart from the main problem under investigation.

Although the above rules have made the results of the study directly comparable with the findings of McCarthy and Day, variations in technique invalidate exact comparison of word frequencies with the results of other investigators. In the Horn list (54) regular plurals and inflected forms, even possessives, are noted separately, and contractions of pronoun and verb are listed as one word. Since Horn gives frequencies of words occurring more than forty times, it is sometimes possible to recompute or combine frequencies, thus sometimes changing the order of importance; but those words having a frequency of less than forty remain an unknown quantity, which might affect the order further. In the Thorndike list (140), on the other hand, regularly formed adverbs are not given ("bad," "badly"), and very few distinctions are made between words used as different parts of speech with very distinct meanings ("like" as verb and as preposition; "mean" as verb and as adjective); furthermore, the Thorndike list contains some unaccountable inconsistencies. The present participle of every verb in the English language is formed by adding the suffix *ing* to the infinitive; yet Thorndike lists "going" and "being" separately, but does not list "having" and "doing." Recomputation and combination is impossible with the Thorndike list, since no exact frequencies are given, and order of importance is the only comparison which can be made.

FINDINGS

Different words. — The total number of different words used by the 436 subjects was 2,033, which is slightly less than the vocabulary given by Smith (122) as that to be expected of a 5-year-old child, and less than half that usually found in a 9-year-old child.* This exceedingly small number of words results of course from the fact that all the language material was obtained in a rather rigidly standardized situation; and as was pointed out above, it could have been predicted before the tabulation of words had proceeded far. Nevertheless there is considerable evidence to indicate that this selection of words is fairly representative of the English language. Since in the final tabulation the words had been arranged alphabetically, it was a simple matter to compare the number beginning with

* According to the standard used in the Stanford-Binet, the vocabulary at 8 years is 3,600 words, and at ten years 5,400 words.

each letter with the corresponding number of pages in the dictionary. This was first done using *Collier's New Dictionary* (1927 edition) of 917 pages containing approximately 32,000 words, and later using the Funk and Wagnalls *Standard Unabridged Dictionary*. The coefficient of correlation (Spearman rank-order formula) in the first instance was .86±.03 and in the second instance .91±.02. Words beginning with *s* were by far the most frequent, the total being 292. The next most frequent were words beginning with *b* and *t*, the total in both cases being 166. In the small dictionary there were 100 pages of *s* words and in the unabridged 300 pages. Second place in the small dictionary went to *a* words and in the unabridged to *c* words. The lead of the *s* words over the others was not so great as in the children's language records.

The ratio of total words to number of different words in the present study as compared with the Zyve (163) and Horn (54)

TABLE 59. — RELATION BETWEEN TOTAL NUMBER OF WORDS USED AND NUMBER OF DIFFERENT WORDS, AS FOUND BY HORN (54), ZYVE (163), AND DAVIS

Investigator	Total Words	Different Words	Ratio
Horn	489,555	7097	69 to 1
Zyve	47,575	2164	22 to 1
Davis	118,004	2033	58 to 1

studies is shown in Table 59. It must be recalled that in the Horn study all inflected forms and contractions were counted as separate words. Zyve does not describe her procedure in this regard, but probably the relatively large number of different words in her study is the result of the diversified topics of conversation. The general trend, however, would seem to be a decrease with age, which is what we should expect as total vocabulary increases. In other words, Horn's kindergarten children have fewer different words to use than do Zyve's third-grade children. The situation in the present study is a standardized one, and therefore the vocabulary is considerably limited, but the results of the Zyve and Horn studies would seem perfectly comparable, since they are derived from free conversation on general topics.

There was also rather close correspondence between the words with the highest frequency and those heading the Horn and Thorndike lists. Of the 2,033 different words, 175 had a frequency of

100 or more, and 23 of the 175 occurred 1,000 or more times. These 175 words are compared with Thorndike's findings in the tabulation below.* The actual words are listed in order of frequency in Appendix IV.

Number of Words	*Position in Thorndike's List*
78	First hundred
31	Second hundred
17	Third hundred
5	Fourth hundred
3	Fifth hundred
17	Second half of first thousand
6	First half of second thousand
4	Second half of second thousand
2	First half of third thousand
1	Second half of third thousand
4	Second five thousand
7	Not found in ten thousand

Smith (122) listed 68 words which were used more than 100 times by her preschool subjects. All except 6 of these ("not," "mine," "train," "your," "sit," and "mama") had a frequency of over 100 in the present study. Moreover, 13 of Smith's 25 most common words, and 16 of Horn's, were among the 25 most common words in the present study. Of the first hundred words, 64 are found in Thorndike's first hundred and 78 in Horn's first hundred. Fourteen of the first hundred words are found in Thorndike's second hundred, 5 in the third hundred, 1 in the fourth, and 1 in the fifth. Six appear in the second five hundred, 4 in the first half of the second thousand, 1 in the second half of the second thousand, 2 ("cowboy" and "buffalo") in the second five thousand. "Uh-huh" and "hm" do not appear at all.

These findings are particularly interesting because a rather specialized vocabulary would be expected in the Wild West situation which was set up. But analysis shows that only about a dozen words are so emphasized as to be greatly displaced from their normal position according to general usage. "Cowboy," "buffalo," "Indian," "gun," "wagon," "oxen," "shoot," "shot," and "bow and arrow" are the only words with a frequency of over 100 which would not ordinarily be found among the thousand most common words. It appears, then, that the great mass of language forms is

---

* Some words were not found in Thorndike's ten thousand. These included "hm," "uh-huh," "anh-anh," "er," "guy," "covered" (adjective), "bow and arrow," although both "bow" and "arrow" appear separately.

virtually unaffected by the specific situation, at least so far as vocabulary is concerned. Dewey (32, page 30), who selected his material in the spring of 1918, noted the same phenomenon in the enhanced importance of some 20 "war words."

FIG. 10. — INCREASE IN NUMBER OF DIFFERENT WORDS USED BY TWINS, SINGLETONS, AND ONLY CHILDREN FROM FIVE AND ONE-HALF TO NINE AND ONE-HALF YEARS

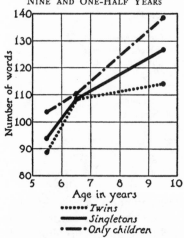

Twins
——— *Singletons*
—•— *Only children*

Group differences in number of words. — Care must be exercised, in discussing the number of words used, to distinguish between data based on the total number of words and data which are based on the number of different words used. In the preceding section of course all words were involved, but in the following analysis the number of different words will be considered. McCarthy's singletons were at every age decidedly superior to Day's twins in number of different words, and an appreciable difference is found at the later ages, particularly in the case of only children. The findings are summarized in Table 60 and are shown graphically in Figure 10.

The increase with age is fairly consistent from year to year for all groups, and is in proportion to the total number of words used. The ratio of different words to total words was calculated for each child, and although the total range was all the way from .20 to .80, the vast majority of indices were about .40, and the index does

TABLE 60. — MEAN NUMBER OF DIFFERENT WORDS USED, AS FOUND BY DAY (31),* McCARTHY (80),† AND DAVIS

Age in Years	Investigator	Twins	Singletons	Only Children
2	Day, McCarthy	20.4	29.1	
3		45.3	62.8	
4		56.5	92.6	
5		65.3		
5½	Davis	88.5	93.9	103.8
6½		108.1	108.2	110.5
9½		114.0	126.3	138.7

* Twins.   † Singletons.

not increase with age. On the contrary, it is .38 for the 9½-year group and .41 for the 5½-year-olds. A similar ratio for the pre-school years may be calculated from the means given by Day and McCarthy. The resulting index at each age for both twins and singletons varies around .40, although it is very slightly higher for singletons than for twins. Probably this constant ratio is another manifestation of the equilibrium between frequency and variety of word usage which Zipf (162) has demonstrated by his standard curve of English.

The relationship between number of different words and IQ, determined by calculating the coefficient of correlation (Pearson

TABLE 61. — MEAN NUMBER OF DIFFERENT WORDS USED BY CHILDREN FROM UPPER AND LOWER OCCUPATIONAL GROUPS

OCCUPATIONAL GROUP	5½-YEAR GROUP			6½-YEAR GROUP			9½-YEAR GROUP		
	Boys	Girls	Both	Boys	Girls	Both	Boys	Girls	Both
Upper . . .	92.4	104.2	98.4	110.7	119.7	115.5	133.0	126.8	129.9
Lower . . .	89.3	90.7	90.0	100.0	105.2	102.4	112.4	124.3	118.5
Both . .	90.7	97.2	93.9	105.0	112.8	108.8	122.4	125.5	123.9

product moment) at each age, proved to be approximately that obtained between length of sentence and IQ. The relationship between word-length ratio and IQ proved very slight, and negative rather than positive. This may mean that the brighter children make greater use of the definite and indefinite articles and are more likely to express the subject and to employ complete verb phrases than the duller children.

Girls at each age use rather more different words than boys, and children from the upper occupational groups more than children from the lower occupational groups. These differences are shown in Table 61.

The standard deviation for the number of different words was not computed except in the 5½-year group, but for this large group the critical ratios were in a number of instances of sufficient magnitude to indicate statistical reliability. The findings are summarized in Table 62.

Length of words. — The tremendous importance of the short word in all languages has long been recognized by students of philology and related subjects. Its frequency is apparent in all word lists which are ranked for frequency, but is more conspicuous in children's lists than in those compiled from adult language or from written material. Zipf (162) reproduces the findings of an analysis of written German made by Kaeding, in which 50 per cent of the words are one syllable in length and 29 per cent are of two syllables. He also cites studies from the Latin of Plautus, from the Chinese, and from newspaper English which agree as to the overwhelming preponderance of short words; but since the German study is the only one which uses the syllable as the unit, and presents its findings in terms of percentage, it has been chosen for purposes of comparison with the present study.

No age nor sex comparisons can be made, since the data for length of word were compiled from the total frequency sheets; but

TABLE 62. — MEAN NUMBER OF WORDS USED BY DIFFERENT GROUPS AT 5½ YEARS

Group	Mean	Group	Mean	Critical Ratio
Boys	90.7	Girls	97.2	2.04
Twins	88.5	Singletons	93.9	1.58
Twins . . . . . . : . .	88.5	Only	103.8	3.63
Singletons	93.9	Only	103.8	2.0
Upper-class girls	104.2	Lower-class girls . . .	90.7	2.91
Articulation perfect . .	102.2	Articulation faulty . .	82.5	5.95

for the 436 subjects at the three age levels, 97.3 per cent of all words used are one and two syllables long. A small source of error is present in the percentage of one-syllable words because inflected forms were not listed separately; hence it is impossible to tell how often a one-syllable word was converted into a two-syllable one by the formation of the present participle, the preterit, or the comparison of adjectives. The percentage of one-syllable words, then, is somewhat too high, and that of two-syllable words somewhat too low, but the combined percentage of 97.3 is approximately accurate. That the error is slight is indicated by a check of the Horn list, in which plurals and all other inflected forms are given, although only for words with a frequency of over 40. The percentage of one-syllable words for kindergarten children, according to the Horn list, is 90.4 and of two-syllable words 9.1. The only four-syllable word with a frequency of over 40 in the Horn list was "kindergarten." In the present study the only true five-syllable word was "electricity," which occurred three times. There were a number of compound words each of which was counted as one five-syllable word, but this was an arbitrary decision. Including "everybody" (7 times), "pencil-sharpener" (4), and "what-you-may-call-it" (4), the total number of five-syllable words was 18. The highly compounded word "whatever-you-call-it," occurring once, was listed as a six-syllable word. The percentages are given in Table 63.

TABLE 63. — PERCENTAGE DISTRIBUTION OF DIFFERENT WORDS USED IN SEVERAL STUDIES ACCORDING TO LENGTH IN SYLLABLES, AS FOUND BY HORN (54), BY KAEDING (160), AND BY DAVIS

Number of Syllables	Davis	Horn	Kaeding
1	92.8	90.4	50.0
2	4.5	9.1	28.9
3	2.4	0.4	12.9
4	0.2	0.03	5.93
5	0.01	0.00	1.72
6	0.001	0.000	0.50
7–15	0.000	0.000	0.22

TABLE 64. — DISTRIBUTION OF 2033 DIFFERENT WORDS USED IN THE PRESENT STUDY ACCORDING TO LENGTH IN SYLLABLES

Number of Syllables	Number of Words	Per Cent
1	1106	54.4
2	696	34.2
3	196	9.6
4	30	1.5
5	4	0.2
6	1	0.05
	2033	99.95

Although the very high percentage of one-syllable words when total words are considered is explained in part because of the great frequency of the articles, pronouns, prepositions, and auxiliary verbs, the preponderance of short words is found when percentages are computed using the number of different words as the base. The figures are presented in Table 64. There were 635 words which occurred only once. When these are tabulated on the basis of syllables of length, it appears that the percentage of longer words increases with infrequency of use, as we should expect from demonstration of the standard curve (162).

Zipf (162) is convinced, and produces evidence for his belief, that in a given sample of language the frequency of occurrence of words is in inverse ratio to the number of words. "The product of the number of words of a given occurrence, when multiplied by the square of their occurrences, remains constant" ($ab^2=k$). This tendency to obtain frequency at the expense of variety of vocabulary may be verified in the data of the present study by inspection, although Zipf says the law is not valid for the most frequent words.

Use of personal pronouns. — Previous students of language development have established the facts that when the long-sentence stage appears, the verb tends to replace the noun as the most used part of speech, adjectives and pronouns are of increasing importance, and prepositions and conjunctions are less often omitted than formerly. Because of this general agreement as to facts, it seemed advisable in the present study to devote more time to the parts of speech which have received less attention, and to omit entirely the classification which has usually been made.

Of all types of pronouns, the personal pronouns are by far the most important. In all the Stormzand (135) material they made up 72.7 per cent of all the pronouns used. The percentage of relative pronouns was 11.9, of indefinite 8.7, of demonstrative 3.9, and of reflexive 1.4, while interrogative, reciprocal, intensive, and identifying pronouns accounted for the remaining 1.6 per cent. From these data he concludes that the declension of pronouns is important and agreement of pronouns with the antecedent should be emphasized, but that the division of pronouns into classes is over-refined. In his material, the use of personal pronouns per sentence decreases slightly with age, from 1.96 in the fourth grade to 1.18 in the eighth, while the average adult ratio is 1.53 personal pronouns per sentence. Markey (84) also reported a great predominance of personal pronouns. He found that "self" pronouns decrease after three years, while other pronouns increase, and believes there is a suggestion in Marston's data (85, page 103) that the use of the second person decreases with age, with a corresponding increase in the use of the first person plural and the third person. Fisher (36) considers the use of the first personal pronoun plural an index of social development. She found a correlation with age of .72, but of only .18 with IQ. Girls, she reports, develop more rapidly than boys in use of this pronoun. Foster * also reports greater use of the first personal pronoun by girls.

* Josephine C. Foster, unpublished research carried on at the Institute of Child Welfare of the University of Minnesota.

Because of the possible age, sex, social, and personality differences in the groups included in the present study, the mean occurrence of personal pronouns by number and person was determined in detail. In the 6½-year group there is a suggestion that twins use the first person singular less often and the first person plural more often than the other children, but since no such difference occurred at the other ages the finding is probably due to the small number of cases in this group. Certain consistent differences are of some significance when related to the total number of personal pronouns.

The mean number of personal pronouns increases with age, is

TABLE 65. — COMPARATIVE USE OF SEVERAL FORMS OF PERSONAL PRONOUNS BY DIFFERENT AGE AND SEX GROUPS

Measure	5½-Year Group			6½-Year Group			9½-Year Group		
	Boys	Girls	Both	Boys	Girls	Both	Boys	Girls	Both
Mean number of first personal pronouns	7.1	8.8	7.9	9.7	11.9	10.8	7.3	7.0	7.2
Mean number of second and third personal pronouns . .	15.9	17.9	16.9	18.8	20.9	19.8	28.3	33.3	30.9
Ratio of first to total second and third	0.45	0.49	0.47	0.51	0.57	0.54	0.26	0.21	0.23
Mean number of possessives	2.2	3.1	2.6	2.6	3.7	3.1	3.2	5.4	4.3
Ratio of possessives to other forms of personal pronouns . .	0.10	0.13	0.12	0.10	0.13	0.11	0.10	0.15	0.13

uniformly greater for girls than for boys, and is greatest of all for only children. At 5½ and 9½ years the number is slightly less for twins than for singletons. The index obtained by relating pronouns of the first person to all other personal pronouns is markedly higher at 5½ and 6½ than at 9½ years. It is slightly higher for girls than for boys at 5½ and 6½ years, but slightly lower at 9½ years. It is highest at each age for only children and lowest for twins, although the differences between groups at 6½ years are negligible. By far the greatest difference is in the 5½-year-old only girls. In this group the ratio is .74, that of twin and singleton girls is .38 and .48, respectively, and that of only boys is .53.

A similar ratio was calculated for the occurrence of the possessive form. There were no age differences, but the index at each age was very slightly higher for girls than for boys and a little lower for only children than for children with siblings. Table 65 shows age and sex differences in the use of the several personal pronouns and of the possessive forms.

Possible differences between twins, singletons with siblings, and only children in the use of the first person and of the possessive form are suggested in Table 79, on page 135. At all ages and in every group there was an enormous preponderance of third person masculine over third person feminine forms, although girls used the feminine more than boys. This is of course in accordance with all language procedure in personification and the use of collective nouns and was inevitable in a situation set up around Indians and cowboys; but it is interesting to find the custom so firmly established at 5½ years. (See Table 66.)

TABLE 66. — COMPARATIVE USE OF THIRD PERSON MASCULINE AND FEMININE FORMS BY DIFFERENT AGE AND SEX GROUPS

MEASURE	5½-YEAR GROUP			6½-YEAR GROUP			9½-YEAR GROUP		
	Boys	Girls	Both	Boys	Girls	Both	Boys	Girls	Both
Mean number masculine	6.8	6.3	6.5	6.6	7.8	7.2	7.9	13.5	10.8
Mean number feminine	0.4	1.5	0.9	0.3	1.2	0.7	0.2	0.9	0.6
Ratio masculine to feminine	0.06	0.24	0.14	0.04	0.15	0.10	0.02	0.07	0.05

Use of definite and indefinite articles. — One suggested explanation of the unexpected lack of relationship between word-length ratio and IQ, discussed above, was a possible tendency for the brighter children to make greater use of the articles. Obviously the child who says "The cow is drinking the milk" is using a higher order of language than he who says "Cow drink milk." In frequency of use by adults "the" always heads the list of words, and the use of the indefinite article is near the top. The frequencies of "a," "an," and "the" have been computed for each group of subjects and the totals expressed in terms of percentage of total speech. The data indicate a slight increase with age in the importance of the articles, as is seen in Table 67. There is a slight absolute difference in the use of the articles in favor of girls and of only children, but this difference does not hold when the totals are related to length of sentence.

Use of conjunctions. — The principal coordinating and subordinating conjunctions were tabulated for frequency of use. The use of conjunctions increases with age, both absolutely and relatively, and is slightly greater for girls than for boys. Coordinating conjunctions are used approximately five times as often as subordinating conjunctions, and the conjunction "and" accounts for 84 per cent of all the coordinating conjunctions at 5½ and 6½ years, and for 88 per

TABLE 67. — COMPARATIVE USE OF ARTICLES BY DIFFERENT AGE AND SEX GROUPS

GROUP	BOYS		GIRLS		BOTH SEXES	
	Mean Number	Percentage of Total Speech	Mean Number	Percentage of Total Speech	Mean Number	Percentage of Total Speech
5½ years.	14.1	6.2	15.1	6.5	14.6	6.3
6½ years.	16.0	6.3	17.9	6.5	16.9	6.4
9½ years.	24.3	7.6	23.7	7.1	24.0	7.3
Twins	17.8	6.9	16.8	6.7	17.4	6.9
Singletons	16.1	6.5	18.4	6.9	17.3	6.7
Only children.	18.3	6.8	18.9	6.2	18.6	6.5

cent at 9½ years. "But" makes up 10 per cent of the total at 5½ years, 11 per cent at 6½, and 5 per cent at 9½ years. "Because," "if," and "though" are the most important subordinating conjunctions. The findings in regard to use of conjunctions are summarized in Table 68 and are given in greater detail in Appendixes V, VI, and VII.

Incidence of slang, colloquialisms, and vulgarity. — This little-studied phase of language has remained practically untouched in investigations of children's language. There is so little agreement among authorities as to the distinction between slang and colloquialisms, provincialisms, and grammatical errors, and the argot changes so rapidly that a compendium such as that of Rose (110) is of doubtful value. Sechrist (117) in 1913 wrote a semi-theoretical article on unconventional language, in which he pointed out many parallels between this and the language of children. Schwesinger (115) reported that a battery of tests on slang given to adolescents in a reformatory showed no correlation between knowledge of slang and degree of delinquency, but she suggested that slang tests might be of value in making comparative studies of social levels. Although

Zyve's (163) material was obtained in a formal school situation, she found 0.4 slang expressions per thousand words.

In the present study colloquialisms and the mild vulgarities common among children have been included in the category of slang. A total of 65 different expressions were used 812 times. The mean number of such expressions was 9 per thousand words at 5½ years and 3 per thousand words at 9½ years. Boys used slang more often than girls, but there was no indication of a difference between upper and lower occupational groups. There is evidence that certain expres-

TABLE 68. — COMPARATIVE USE OF CONJUNCTIONS BY DIFFERENT AGE AND SEX GROUPS

MEASURE	5½-YEAR GROUP			6½-YEAR GROUP			9½-YEAR GROUP		
	Boys	Girls	Both	Boys	Girls	Both	Boys	Girls	Both
Coordinating conjunctions									
Mean number	3.0	5.3	4.2	5.8	6.7	6.2	11.1	14.7	12.9
Percentage of total speech	1.3	2.2	1.8	2.3	2.4	2.3	3.5	4.4	4.0
Subordinating conjunctions									
Mean number	0.5	0.9	0.7	1.3	1.3	1.3	2.5	3.0	2.6
Percentage of total speech	0.2	0.4	0.3	0.5	0.5	0.5	0.8	0.9	0.7
Both types									
Mean number	3.5	6.2	4.9	7.1	8.0	7.5	13.6	17.6	15.6
Percentage of total speech	1.5	2.6	2.1	2.8	2.9	2.8	4.2	5.2	4.7
"And"									
Mean number	2.5	4.5	3.5	5.1	5.4	5.2	9.3	13.5	11.4
Percentage of total speech	1.1	1.9	1.5	2.0	2.0	2.0	2.9	4.0	3.5
"But"									
Mean number	0.3	0.5	0.4	0.5	0.9	0.7	0.7	0.5	0.6
Percentage of total speech	0.1	0.2	0.2	0.2	0.3	0.3	0.2	0.1	0.2

sions ("guy," "yeah," "boy," "gosh," "heck") are characteristic of boys, while "cute" was used only 3 times by boys, but 32 times by girls.

SUMMARY

1. There were 2,033 different words used by the 436 subjects.

2. Nearly all the words of high frequency are also of high frequency in word lists obtained by other investigators.

3. The number of different words increases with age and is greater for girls than for boys and for children from the upper than from the lower occupational classes.

4. Twins at each age use the smallest number of different words

and only children use the greatest. At 5½ years this difference is statistically reliable.

5. The ratio between number of different words and total number of words does not vary with age, but is slightly higher for singletons and only children than for twins.

6. About 97 per cent of all the words used are one and two syllables in length.

7. The use of personal pronouns increases with age, is greater for girls than for boys, and is greater for only children than for other children. The ratio of pronouns of the first person to other personal pronouns decreases with age.

8. The use of the definite and indefinite articles increases with age.

9. The use of conjunctions increases with age and is slightly greater for girls than for boys.

10. Younger children and boys use more slang expressions than older children and girls. Certain expressions seem to be characteristic of the language of boys, and others are favored by girls.

VIII. TYPES OF TWINS AND RESEMBLANCES BETWEEN TWIN PAIRS

TYPES OF TWINS

For the purposes of the present study, classification of the twins as to identity or nonidentity was considered of only incidental importance. When the information was readily available it was recorded, but no consultations with physicians or ransacking of hospital records was undertaken. The distribution of the 83 sets of twins is given in Table 69. Three of the six sets of identical twins were among Day's subjects.

If we accept Dahlberg's (28) estimate that about 38 per cent of like-sex pairs are identical, 16 of the sets listed as uncertain are identical; but there is no basis whatever for making a determination. Since these 24 pairs are so much alike that there is a possibility of identity, it would seem probable, however, that this group would show nearly as great a resemblance between pairs in the various comparisons possible from the data as the identical sets, and an appreciably greater resemblance than the clearly fraternal pairs.

AMOUNT OF DIFFERENCE BETWEEN THE INDIVIDUALS MAKING UP TWIN PAIRS

For purposes of comparison it was decided to take the mean difference between pairs for each type of twin in five distinct phases of test and linguistic behavior, all of which permit an objective and highly diagnostic statement of results. These are IQ, length of time necessary to secure fifty remarks, length of sentence, number of spontaneous remarks, and number of different words. As a simple check upon the importance of the findings, a similar mean was obtained for the same number of unrelated pairs of non-only singletons of the same age, sex, and occupational class. This was readily done by juxtaposition on the large summary sheets for each trait. In general the differences are appreciably greater for the unrelated pairs; consequently there appears to be justification for attaching some significance to the findings, which indicate on the whole a tendency toward greater resemblance between identical than fraternal twins. The conflicting results when like-sex twins are compared with unlike-sex twins seem to indicate less resemblance for unlike-sex pairs in IQ and spontaneity of speech, but somewhat greater resemblance in length of time required, and considerably greater resemblance in the purely linguistic traits. It must be remembered, however, that there is greater possibility of sampling errors in the case of unlike-sex twins, since their number is only 23. The results of the comparisons are summarized in Table 70.

When these comparisons are made on the basis of age, there appears to be a tendency in twin pairs for differences to increase with age in length of sentence, number of different words, and number of spontaneous remarks. Unrelated pairs, on the other hand, are practically as different at 5½ years in the number of different words used and in the number of spontaneous remarks as they are at 9½ years, and the difference in sentence length, which triples for twins, increases for unrelated pairs only from 1.7 words at 5½ to 2.4 at 9½ years. This seems to be very convincing evidence of the importance of early association in developing language habits. The findings for the three age groups are given in Table 71.

Comparison of Like- and Unlike-Sex Pairs

Articulation. — A particularly striking difference between twin pairs was found in studying the articulation of twins at the kinder-

Fig. 11. — Percentage of Like-Sex and Unlike-Sex Twins Having Perfect Articulation at Five and One-Half Years

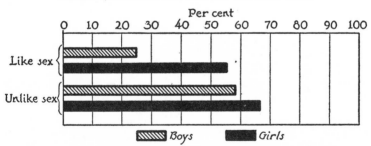

garten age. As was pointed out in Chapter III, twins of this age are much more likely to retain infantile pronunciations and minor speech difficulties than singletons and only children, and boys are more prone to faulty articulation than girls. But further analysis shows that this finding does not hold true for the boys in unlike-sex pairs. Only 25 per cent of like-sex boy twins have perfect articulation, as compared with 58.3 per cent of boys in unlike-sex pairs. The difference is especially noticeable in the lower occupational

TABLE 69. — DISTRIBUTION OF 83 TWIN PAIRS ACCORDING TO TYPE OF TWIN

AGE IN YEARS	IDENTICAL			UNCERTAIN			FRATERNAL LIKE-SEX			ALL LIKE-SEX			UNLIKE-SEX
	Boys	Girls	Both	Boys	Girls	Both	Boys	Girls	Both	Boys	Girls	Both	
5½	1	3	4	10	5	15	7	10	17	18	18	36	12
6½	1	1	2	1	1	2	2	2	4	4	4	8	3
9½	0	0	0	2	5	7	6	3	9	8	8	16	8
Total	2	4	6	13	11	24	15	15	30	30	30	60	23

TABLE 70. — MEAN DIFFERENCES BETWEEN TWINS AND UNRELATED PAIRS OF SINGLETONS IN FIVE SELECTED TRAITS

TRAIT	TWINS								UNRELATED PAIRS				
	Identical	Uncertain	Fraternal Like-Sex	All Like-Sex			Unlike-Sex	All Twins	Boys	Girls	Both	Unlike-Sex	All
				Boys	Girls	Both							
Points IQ	8.2	7.4	11.8	12.2	7.5	9.7	12.4	10.5	16.7	13.8	15.2	16.9	15.6
Minutes required for test	6.5	7.2	5.7	6.7	6.1	6.4	5.6	6.2	6.7	6.9	6.8	6.8	6.8
Words per sentence	1.1	1.3	1.8	1.2	1.9	1.5	.8	1.3	1.7	2.1	1.9	2.0	1.9
Number of spontaneous remarks	4.2	10.2	7.4	6.9	9.4	8.2	10.1	8.7	11.8	17.0	14.4	18.3	15.5
Number of different words	10.3	22.8	23.6	21.1	22.8	22.0	17.3	20.7	28.9	34.9	31.9	27.9	30.8

TABLE 71. — MEAN DIFFERENCES BETWEEN TWINS AND UNRELATED PAIRS OF SINGLETONS IN FIVE SELECTED TRAITS AT THREE AGE LEVELS

Age and Trait	Twins								Unrelated Pairs				
	Identical	Uncertain	Fraternal Like-Sex	All Like-Sex			Unlike-Sex	All	Boys	Girls	Both	Unlike-Sex	All
				Boys	Girls	Both							
5½ years													
IQ	6.2	8.1	11.5	10.9	8.0	9.5	16.0	11.1	18.6	17.1	17.9	16.2	17.5
Minutes required	3.7	7.4	6.7	7.2	6.1	6.7	4.5	6.1	5.5	6.5	6.0	8.5	6.7
Words per sentence	1.0	0.8	1.0	0.6	1.4	1.0	0.5	0.8	1.4	2.1	1.7	1.8	1.7
Number of spontaneous remarks	3.5	6.1	7.9	6.8	6.5	6.7	4.0	6.0	9.7	15.5	12.6	23.0	15.2
Total words	11.0	18.5	17.3	13.8	20.4	17.1	11.7	15.7	21.9	36.2	29.1	32.3	29.9
6½ years													
IQ	12.0	7.0	9.2	12.5	6.2	9.4	9.3	9.4	15.7	7.7	11.7	14.7	12.5
Minutes required	12.0	8.0	3.0	8.2	4.7	6.5	6.7	6.5	10.0	9.7	9.9	7.3	9.2
Words per sentence	1.1	1.2	1.7	1.4	1.0	1.2	0.9	1.1	1.8	2.2	2.0	1.2	1.8
Number of spontaneous remarks	5.5	13.5	1.7	3.0	8.2	5.6	10.0	6.8	11.5	13.0	12.2	6.0	10.5
Total words	9.0	15.5	25.2	14.2	23.2	18.7	21.0	19.4	34.0	39.7	36.9	17.7	31.6
9½ years													
IQ	.....	6.0	18.4	15.0	7.0	10.4	8.2	9.6	9.7	7.2	8.3	18.7	12.1
Minutes required	.....	6.4	5.0	4.6	6.6	5.6	7.0	6.1	7.5	6.2	6.9	4.1	5.9
Words per sentence	.....	2.3	3.6	2.4	3.6	3.0	1.3	2.5	2.5	2.2	2.4	2.6	2.4
Number of spontaneous remarks	.....	18.0	8.8	9.1	16.5	12.8	19.4	15.0	16.6	22.4	19.5	16.0	18.3
Total words	.....	34.3	34.7	41.0	28.0	34.5	24.4	31.1	42.1	29.6	35.9	25.0	32.2

groups, where only 10 per cent of the like-sex boys are free from this handicap, although 57.1 per cent of the boys in unlike-sex pairs are rated as perfect. This suggests that the twin sister, developing a little faster than the boy, may act as a pacemaker for him; but it is equally possible that unlike-sex twins because of parental attitude or differing interests are less dependent on each other than twins of the same sex and more likely to seek out the wider contacts which

TABLE 72. — PERCENTAGE OF 5½-YEAR-OLD LIKE- AND UNLIKE-SEX
TWINS FROM UPPER AND LOWER OCCUPATIONAL GROUPS WHO
HAD PERFECT ARTICULATION

OCCUPATIONAL GROUP	LIKE-SEX			UNLIKE-SEX		
	Boys	Girls	Both	Boys	Girls	Both
Upper	43.7	66.7	55.9	60.0	60.0	60.0
Lower	10.0	44.4	26.3	57.1	71.4	64.3
Both	25.0	55.5	40.3	58.3	66.7	62.5

stimulate and facilitate attempts at articulate speech. The percentage of like- and unlike-sex twins having perfect articulation at 5½ years is shown in Table 72. This comparison is made graphically in Figure 11.

Not only do like-sex boy twins tend to have speech defects more frequently than boys in unlike-sex pairs, but there is evidence indicating that if one member of such a pair has difficulty with articulation, his brother is likely to have it also. Girl pairs are about as likely to be both perfect as both faulty, and the chances are equal that one member of the pair will have a defect when the other does not. Among unlike-sex pairs both members are defective in a smaller percentage of cases than in any other combination. In the 5½-year group, where most of the speech difficulty is centered, faulty articulation in twins is distributed as shown in Table 73. Of the pairs

TABLE 73. — DISTRIBUTION OF FAULTY ARTICULATION AMONG
48 SETS OF TWINS AT 5½ YEARS

	BOTH PERFECT		BOTH FAULTY		ONE FAULTY	
	Number	Per Cent	Number	Per Cent	Number	Per Cent
Both boys	3	16.7	14	77.8	1	5.5
Both girls	7	38.8	5	27.8	6	33.3
Unlike-sex	5	41.7	2	16.6	5	41.7

in which both members are similarly classified as to articulation (that is, both perfect or both faulty), 17 pairs (94.5 per cent) are both males, 12 (66.7 per cent) are females, and 7 (58.3 per cent) are unlike. Of the pairs in which one member is perfect, the other faulty, 1 (5.5 per cent) consists of two males, 6 (33.3 per cent) of two females, and 5 (41.7 per cent) of unlike-sex twins. The contrast may be further demonstrated by comparing the percentage of males with faulty articulation in the all-male group with that in all other groups. We find that 29 males or 80.3 per cent of the all-

TABLE 74. — MEAN NUMBER OF WORDS PER REMARK USED BY LIKE- AND UNLIKE-SEX TWINS FROM UPPER AND LOWER OCCUPATIONAL GROUPS

GROUP	UNLIKE-SEX			LIKE-SEX		
	Boys	Girls	Both	Boys	Girls	Both
5½ years						
Upper occupational . . .	4.90	4.69	4.79	4.65	4.67	4.66
Lower occupational . . .	4.72	4.71	4.71	4.16	3.91	4.03
Both	4.79	4.70	4.74	4.38	4.29	4.33
6½ years						
Upper occupational . . .	7.46	5.96	6.71	5.39	5.95	5.67
Lower occupational . . .	4.89	4.89	4.89	5.34	4.69	5.01
Both	5.74	5.18	5.46	5.37	5.32	5.34
9½ years						
Upper occupational . . .	6.26	4.89	5.57	7.76	8.35	8.05
Lower occupational . . .	5.04	5.85	5.44	5.40	4.46	4.93
Both	5.65	5.37	5.51	6.68	6.29	6.48
All ages						
Upper occupational . . .	5.70	4.90	5.30	5.70	5.82	5.76
Lower occupational . . .	4.85	5.09	4.97	4.62	4.17	4.39
Both	5.22	5.00	5.11	5.12	5.00	5.06

male group are faulty, but only 5 or 41.7 per cent of the males in the male-female group. In the all-female group, on the other hand, 16 or 44.4 per cent are faulty, and 4 or 33.3 per cent of the females in the male-female group.

Although any attempts to explain these findings are pure speculation, the phenomena may result from the perfect satisfaction experienced by a small boy in the companionship of his twin brother, and the mother's consequent willingness to leave them absorbed in the mechanical and constructive activities which are so foreign to her understanding.

Sentence length. — Table 74 compares like- and unlike-sex twins at each age in length of sentence. Apparently at the 5½-year level boys in unlike-sex pairs use slightly longer sentences than do boys with twins of the same sex, but the advantage seems to have disappeared by the age of 9½. The same advantage is suggested in girls of the lower occupational groups at all ages, but in the upper occupational groups there is no difference except at 9½ years, when the advantage is definitely in favor of the like-sex group.

A similar comparison of like- and unlike-sex twins in both absolute and relative variability of sentence length shows little difference for girls, but indicates that the 5½- and 6½-year-old unlike-sex boys are more variable than the like-sex boys, while the reverse is true at 9½ years.

TABLE 75. — MEAN IQ OF LIKE-SEX AND UNLIKE-SEX TWINS FROM UPPER AND LOWER OCCUPATIONAL GROUPS

Group	Boys		Girls	
	Like-Sex	Unlike-Sex	Like-Sex	Unlike-Sex
5½ years				
Upper occupational	100.8	111.2	100.8	114.0
Lower occupational	91.4	97.9	96.3	104.7
Both	95.6	103.4	98.6	108.6
6½ years				
Upper occupational	106.7	124.0	106.7	109.0
Lower occupational	98.7	101.5	107.0	108.0
Both	102.7	109.0	106.9	108.3
9½ years				
Upper occupational	118.2	115.0	113.9	113.7
Lower occupational	95.3	107.5	115.4	105.7
Both	108.4	111.2	115.2	109.7

Intelligence. — In the 5½- and 6½-year groups the IQ of unlike-sex twins from both upper and lower occupational classes proved a number of points higher than that of like-sex twins. This is also true of 9½-year-old boys from the lower occupational classes. Day's mean IQ for 88 like-sex twins was 93.5, and for 35 unlike-sex twins 96.2. The distribution for the present study is given in Table 75.

Spontaneity of speech. — Unlike-sex twins also tended to make their fifty remarks in a slightly shorter time than like-sex twins, and at 5½ years a larger number of their responses were spontaneous.

Number of different words. — Unlike-sex twins in the two younger age groups use more different words than like-sex twins, but the tendency is not consistent except for children from the lower occupational classes. At 9½ years like-sex twins use more different words than unlike-sex twins, except for boys from the lower occupational groups.

Miscellaneous Resemblances and Differences in Twin Pairs

Adjustment to school. — One incidental result of the contact with the schools necessary in order to locate the requisite twin pairs was the discovery that certain definite problems connected with twins are well recognized by teachers and principals. These may be listed here, as suggestive of further research, although there is as yet little quantitative evidence in support or refutation of the general belief.

1. *Initial shyness.* — Twins often experience exceptional difficulty in adjusting to school. Over a long period of time independent reports have been noted from speech teachers, school nurses, and even mothers attending child study classes, regarding twins at the W——— school who cried all the time, or who even at the close of the school year would not go to the nurse's room singly. Such pairs were girls more often than boys, and were never of unlike sex. The individual classroom teacher, in discussing her particular twins, would frequently say, "I'm surprised that they went with you at all"; or, "Three weeks ago they wouldn't have said a word."

2. *Emotional interdependence.* — Not only are many twins at the age of school entrance completely lost without each other's constant companionship, but there is evidence that only gradually do they become aware of an individual identity. One set of first-grade boys considered it perfectly fair for *both* of them to fight *one* enemy. If one twin masters the multiplication table and the other does not, the slow one may refuse to make further effort, since Jimmie knows it. Or Jane cannot see that it is cheating for her to fly out of her seat to help John with his test. More serious is the torture suffered when the twin meets with punishment for misconduct.

3. *Irregular attendance.* — If one twin is ill, it is the exception rather than the rule during the early school years for the other to come to school. Here again this condition is most common in girl pairs, and least common in unlike-sex pairs.

4. *Parental sentimentality.* — The above problems would be much simplified were it not for the insistence of parents that twins be in the same class. Even in cases of marked difference in ability, mothers are usually extremely reluctant to have them separated. Both members of all sets of the 5½- and 6½-year-old twins were in the same room except one set of boys who had been adopted into

different homes, and in most instances they were dressed alike and sat side by side. Of the 24 pairs of 9½-year-old twins, 15 were still in the same grade, although one set of boys were in different rooms.

The distribution of the 9½-year group is given in the tabulation below. A further suggestion as to the great importance in the twin's world of the fact of his twinship may be obtained by comparing the frequency of the word "twin" in the speech of twins and of other children. The word appears in Thorndike's third thousand, but the frequency for the twins in the present study was 25, and for other children 8.

Placement	Both Boys	Both Girls	Unlike-Sex
Same grade	4	7	4
Different grade	4	1	4

SUMMARY

1. Twins are more alike than unrelated pairs matched for sex and occupational group in IQ, length of sentence, number of different words, number of spontaneous remarks, and time required to obtain fifty remarks.

2. Identical twins are more alike than other twins.

3. The amount of difference between twins increases with age, but the difference between unrelated pairs is practically the same at all ages.

4. Unlike-sex twins are more alike in some traits than like-sex twins, but less alike in others.

5. At 5½ years 58 per cent of boys in unlike-sex pairs have achieved perfect articulation, as compared with only 25 per cent of boys in like-sex pairs. Among girls of the same age the difference is in the same direction, but is much less. Both members have faulty articulation in 78 per cent of boy pairs, 28 per cent of girl pairs, and 17 per cent of unlike-sex pairs. The articulation of the two members is similar in 94 per cent of boy pairs, 67 per cent of girl pairs, and 58 per cent of unlike-sex pairs.

6. At 5½ and 6½ years the mean sentence length, number of different words, and readiness of response are somewhat greater for unlike-sex than for like-sex twins.

7. The mean IQ of unlike-sex twins at 5½ and 6½ years is approximately seven points higher than that of like-sex twins.

IX. CONCLUSIONS

GENERAL SUMMARY

The analysis of fifty remarks obtained under a standardized situation from each of 436 children between the ages of 5½ and 9½ years has made possible a number of group comparisons and the tracing of several developmental trends. Three discrete age groups of twins, singletons with siblings, and only children have been selected on the basis of paternal occupation to be representative of the Minneapolis–St. Paul population. For the most part, the methodology, both in the conduct of the investigation and in types of analysis, has been that devised by McCarthy and followed by Day, and whenever possible direct comparison has been made with the findings of the two earlier studies. Nevertheless this investigation in no sense duplicates the former ones. The greater chronological age of the subjects and the inclusion of only children necessitated a shift of emphasis to certain phases of language development which were not significant during the preschool period. It has been assumed that the reliability of the method has been satisfactorily demonstrated not only by McCarthy and Day but by the subsequent work of McConnon.

Instead of classifying the percentage of remarks at each age which were comprehensible, as was necessary with preschool children, the procedure has been to rate the subjects for the degree of perfection of articulation. It was then possible to study the length, function, complexity, and perfection of remarks and the extent of vocabulary in relation to articulation as well as to chronological age, sex, paternal occupation, and sibling relationship.

At all ages, and for all groups, there was wide individual variation in the mastery of language. A number of children in the 5½-year group exceeded the performance of some subjects in the 9½-year group, and one or two kindergartners exceeded the mean performance of the fourth graders. In the same way there was much overlapping when comparisons were made on the basis of sex, occupational groups, and sibling relationship. Group differences, however, were clear cut, and in general were in keeping with those found in previous investigations. In the sections which follow, quan-

TABLE 76. — SUMMARY OF DIFFERENCES IN LANGUAGE USAGE AT 5½ AND 9½ YEARS

Measure	5½-Year Group	9½-Year Group
Percentage having perfect articulation	65	91
Mean number of words per remark	4.6	6.5
Correlation between IQ and mean length of remark	0.48 *	0.20 †
Percentage of single-word expressions	21.0	15.3
Mean individual *SD* of sentence length	2.79	4.22
Minutes required for test.	12.75	15.09
Percentage of answers	22	33
Percentage of questions	12	4
Percentage of emotionally toned remarks.	4	2
Percentage of simple sentences without phrase	30	20
Percentage of elaborated sentences	4	11
Mean number of subordinate clauses per 1000 words. . . .	19	28
Subordination index (after LaBrant).	0.10	0.17
Mean number of infinitives per 1000 words.	7	15
Mean number of auxiliary verbs per 1000 words	57	67
Mean errors per 1000 words (exclusive of omissions). . . .	32	22
Mean error index (including omissions — after Smith) . . .	0.06	0.05
Mean number of different words	94	124
Mean ratio of different words to total words	0.41	0.38
Percentage of articles	6.3	7.3
Percentage of conjunctions	2.1	4.7
Percentage of conjunction "and"	1.5	3.5
Pronoun index	0.47	0.23
Incidence of slang per 1000 words	9	3

* *PE* = .03.   † *PE* = .06.

titative expressions of consistent group differences are reproduced to indicate the trend of evidence.

LANGUAGE DEVELOPMENT AT 5½ COMPARED WITH THAT AT 9½

Just as has been found in preschool children, the trend with advancing chronological age is definitely toward better articulation, longer and more complex sentences, and the use of a larger vocabulary. Mental growth is indicated by the expression of precise relationships and shades of meaning with the help of pronouns, articles, conjunctions, prepositions, and auxiliary verbs, while grammatical errors tend to decrease. Questions and emotionally toned remarks decrease with age. There is some evidence to show that answers increase with age, but this may be the case only for the situation in which these data were obtained. It is quite probable that the simple situation which so successfully stimulated spontaneous remarks, curiosity, questions, and affective reactions in

TABLE 77. — SUMMARY OF SEX DIFFERENCES IN LINGUISTIC SKILL

Measure	Boys	Girls
Minutes required	13.56	14.15
Percentage having perfect articulation at 5½	56	73
Percentage having perfect articulation at 9½	87	95
Substitutions of d for th	429	214
Substitutions of w for r	81	32
Substitutions of t, th for s	3	78
Mean number of words per remark, upper class	5.38	5.66
Mean number of words per remark, lower class	4.90	5.06
Mean number of words per remark, both classes	5.13	5.35
Mean individual SD of sentence length	3.13	3.43
Percentage of single-word expressions	18.0	19.6
Percentage of answers	20.9	28.0
Percentage of questions	10.3	8.4
Percentage of emotionally toned remarks	2.9	4.1
Percentage of elaborated sentences	5.8	6.7
Mean number of infinitives per 1000 words	9.1	10.5
Mean number of auxiliary verbs per 1000 words	59	62
Mean number of errors per 1000 words	28	25
Mean number of different words	102	107
Pronoun index	0.41	0.42
Percentage of conjunctions	2.8	3.6
Incidence of slang per 1000 words	9	6

younger children produced hesitation and indecision at 9½ years because it was so foreign to the usual school experience. Much of the somewhat egocentric monologue of the kindergartner has by this age given way to internal speech, and the fourth grader has long since learned that most of one's talking in school is expected to be limited to answering questions.

At each age nearly 20 per cent of all remarks are of only one word. About 70 per cent of the emotionally toned remarks and 40 per cent of answers are of this length. Although the number of functionally complete but structurally incomplete sentences decreases with age, the number of incomplete sentences does not. It seems probable that this finding, like the increase in number of answers, is related to social experience rather than to mental growth. Certainly the casual conversation of adults is far from free from laconic and elliptical remarks. Table 76 summarizes in quantitative terms the differences in linguistic skill at 5½ and 9½ years.

SEX DIFFERENCES IN LINGUISTIC SKILL

In nearly every phase of language studied, girls were found to retain up to the 9½-year level the superiority which has been previously demonstrated for the preschool period. This is true of articulation, word usage, and length, complexity, and grammatical correctness of sentences. Girls use more personal pronouns and conjunctions than boys, and less slang. Boys show greater spontaneity of speech and ask more questions, but this may result from personality traits and differential training rather than from differences in command of language. In general, sex differences are greater in children from the lower than in those from the upper occupational

TABLE 78. — SUMMARY OF DIFFERENCES BETWEEN CHILDREN FROM THE UPPER AND LOWER OCCUPATIONAL GROUPS IN LINGUISTIC SKILL

Measure	Upper Occupational Group	Lower Occupational Group
Minutes required for test.	13.25	14.83
Percentage having perfect articulation at 5½	73	58
Percentage having perfect articulation at 9½	93	89
Mean number of words per remark	5.51	4.98
Mean individual SD of sentence length	3.53	3.05
Percentage of single-word expressions	16.9	20.6
Percentage of answers	20.8	27.7
Percentage of questions	10.6	8.2
Percentage of emotionally toned remarks.	3.9	3.1
Percentage of functionally complete, structurally incomplete remarks.	32.7	37.6
Percentage of elaborated sentences	7.2	5.3
Mean number of subordinate clauses per 1000 words.	24.9	20.1
Subordination index (after LaBrant).	.15	.11
Mean number of errors per 1000 words.	25	29
Mean number of different words	110	100

groups. The superiority of only girls is especially marked.* Sex differences in language development and usage are summarized in Table 77.

DIFFERENCES IN LINGUISTIC SKILL IN DIFFERENT OCCUPATIONAL GROUPS

Children from the upper occupational groups are definitely superior to children from the lower occupational groups in every phase of language ability. They also display greater spontaneity of speech. In general, the difference between upper- and lower-class girls is greater than the difference between upper- and lower-class boys. Table 78 summarizes these tendencies.

* This finding is discussed in detail in E. A. Davis, "The Mental and Linguistic Superiority of Only Girls," *Child Development*, 8: 139–43 (June, 1937).

LANGUAGE USAGE BY TWINS, SINGLETONS, AND ONLY CHILDREN

Twins of 5½ years are decidedly inferior to other children in articulation. More defects were found in boys than in girls, and more in like-sex boy pairs than in either boys or girls in unlike-sex pairs. The inferiority is especially marked in twins from the lower occupational groups. In other phases of language development the performance of twins from the upper occupational groups is very similar to that of other children, but in twins from the lower occu-

TABLE 79. — SUMMARY OF DIFFERENCES BETWEEN TWINS, SINGLETONS, AND ONLY CHILDREN IN LINGUISTIC SKILL

Measure	Twins	Singletons	Only Children
Minutes required.	13.7	14.5	13.1
Percentage having perfect articulation at 5½ . . .	46	76	79
Percentage having perfect articulation at 9½ . . .	87	90	100
Mean number of words per remark	5.07	5.12	5.73
Mean individual SD of sentence length	3.08	3.20	3.74
Percentage of single-word responses	17.8	20.2	16.8
Percentage of answers	23.7	28.6	18.3
Percentage of questions	9.7	8.4	10.3
Percentage of emotionally toned remarks	3.3	3.0	4.7
Percentage of elaborated sentences	5.3	5.8	8.8
Mean number of subordinate clauses per 1000 words	20	21.6	27.5
Subordination index	0.11	0.12	0.16
Mean number of auxiliary verbs per 1000 words . .	59	61	62
Mean number of different words	98.5	105.6	114.1
Pronoun index	0.37	0.41	0.49
Possessive pronoun index	0.14	0.12	0.10

pational groups the inferiority to other children is in some instances greater at 9½ than at 5½ years. This indicates that twins who enjoy a favorable environment tend to overcome the language handicap which is characteristic of the preschool period, but that in under-privileged twins the handicap persists at least up to the age of 9½ years. In most of the quantitative findings given in Table 79 the differences between twins and other children would be considerably greater if the comparisons were made only for subjects drawn from the lower occupational groups.

Except in articulatory difficulty, singletons with siblings appear to resemble twins in language ability more closely than they resemble only children. Apparently the presence of siblings, irrespective of twinship, operates so as to impede maximum progress toward adult command of language. The relative standing of twins, singletons, and only children in those phases of language development which seem to indicate possible differences is given in Table 79. The singletons more than twins or only children lacked spontaneity of speech.

In Figures 12 and 13 the findings of the present study have been

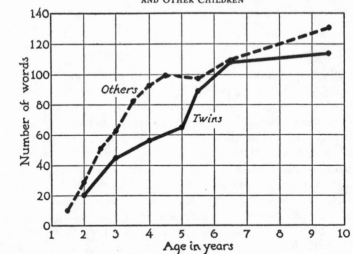

FIG. 12. — MEAN LENGTH OF RESPONSE FOR TWINS AND OTHER CHILDREN

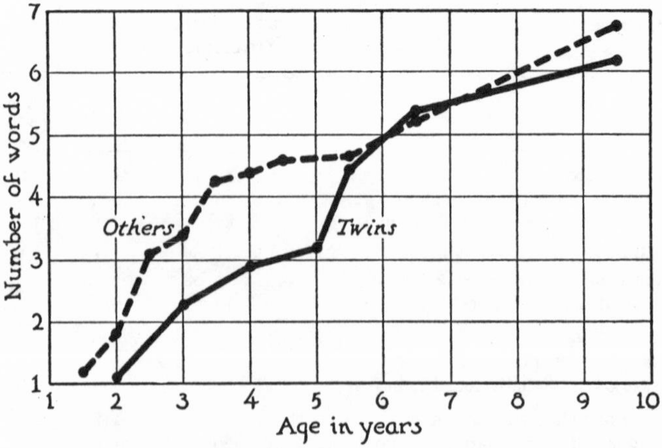

FIG. 13. — MEAN NUMBER OF DIFFERENT WORDS USED BY TWINS AND OTHER CHILDREN

integrated with those of Day and McCarthy for two highly objective measures of language development — mean length of remark and mean number of different words. For this presentation the only children and singletons with siblings have been grouped, as was done in the McCarthy study, and compared with twins. The curve representing this combined group is labeled "others." The difference between twins and singletons ("others") is slight at 5½ years and the curves come together at 6½ years, but at 9½ years there is again a small difference. There is a decided spurt in twins between the ages of 5 and 5½ years, for which the most logical explanation is the stimulation of the enriched linguistic environment which they have enjoyed during their six months of kindergarten experience.

CONCLUSIONS

The findings of this study seem to warrant the following general conclusions:

1. Only children are definitely superior to children with siblings in every phase of linguistic skill.

2. Singletons with siblings are in turn somewhat superior to twins.

3. Twins from the upper occupational groups by 9½ years have practically overcome their language handicap, but twins from the lower occupational groups have made relatively little progress. This finding necessitates careful control of the socio-economic factor in subsequent studies dealing with language development in twins.

4. Twins of the ages studied in this investigation are especially retarded in perfection of articulation. The inferiority is marked during the kindergarten period, particularly in twins from the lower occupational groups.

5. At least during the kindergarten year, a child's mastery of articulation is closely related to other phases of language development. There are indications in the data that faulty articulation, if unduly prolonged, may become a major handicap preventing both adequate command of language and wholesome development of the personality.

APPENDIX I

List of Schools from Which Subjects Were Selected

MINNEAPOLIS

Agassiz	McKinley	
Audubon	Madison	
Barton	Mann	
Bremer	Minnehaha	
Burroughs	Monroe	
Cary	Motley	
Clay	Page	
Cleveland	Penn	
Clinton	Pillsbury	
Corcoran	Pratt	
Douglas	Rosedale	
Emerson	St. Bridgets'	
Ericson	St. Laurence's	
Field	Schiller	
Grant	Seward	
Harrison	Simmons	
Hawthorne	Standish	
Hiawatha	Stowe	
Holland	Van Cleve	
Howe	Washington	
Johnson	Webster	
Longfellow	Whittier	
Lowell	Willard	

ST. PAUL

Adams
Bryant
Davis
Galtier
Gordon
Hancock
Hill
Homecroft
Jefferson
LaFayette
Linwood Park
Longfellow
McKinley
Mattocks
Mounds Park
Riverside
St. Francis
St. Mark's
St. Matthew's
Tatum
Van Buren

APPENDIX II

Distribution of Cases in the Several Occupational Groups

Occupational Group	Age in Years	Twins			Singletons			Only			All		
		Boys	Girls	Both	Boys	Girls	Both	Boys	Girls	Both	Boys	Girls	Both
I	5½	3	1	4	3	3	6	2	2	4	8	6	14
	6½	0	2	2	1	1	2	0	0	0	1	3	4
	9½	1	1	2	1	1	2	1	0	1	3	2	5
	Total	4	4	8	5	5	10	3	2	5	12	11	23
II	5½	5	3	8	3	3	6	2	1	3	10	7	17
	6½	2	0	2	0	1	1	1	1	2	3	2	5
	9½	3	1	4	2	2	4	1	2	3	6	5	11
	Total	10	4	14	5	6	11	4	4	8	19	14	33
III	5½	13	19	32	18	17	35	9	10	19	40	46	86
	6½	3	3	6	4	4	8	4	4	8	11	11	22
	9½	8	10	18	9	9	18	4	4	8	21	23	44
	Total	24	32	56	31	30	61	17	18	35	72	80	152
Total upper		38	40	78	41	41	82	24	24	48	103	105	208
V	5½	17	13	30	12	13	25	7	8	15	36	34	70
	6½	3	3	6	3	2	5	2	2	4	8	7	15
	9½	6	6	12	7	7	14	3	3	6	16	16	32
	Total	26	22	48	22	22	44	12	13	25	60	57	117
VI	5½	8	8	16	8	8	16	4	4	8	20	20	40
	6½	2	0	2	2	2	4	2	2	4	6	4	10
	9½	3	3	6	4	4	8	3	2	5	10	9	19
	Total	13	11	24	14	14	28	9	8	17	36	33	69
VII	5½	2	4	6	5	6	11	3	1	4	10	11	21
	6½	1	3	4	1	1	2	1	0	1	3	4	7
	9½	3	3	6	3	3	6	0	2	2	6	8	14
	Total	6	10	16	9	10	19	4	3	7	19	23	42
Total lower		45	43	88	45	46	91	25	24	49	115	113	228

APPENDIX III
Ratings on Behavior during the Test

Shyness

1. Child comes to examining room readily, talks freely, seems entirely at ease throughout test.
2. Child shows some hesitation at first, but does not cry or seem frightened. After a few minutes' acquaintance is entirely willing to remain with examiner and appears to be completely at ease thereafter.
3. Child requires much persuasion before he can be induced to remain in the room without his mother. Eventually yields, but continues to show anxiety as to mother's whereabouts; has to be reassured frequently. May cry a little at the outset.
4. Child cannot be persuaded to remain in examining room without mother. With mother present, goes through the tests in a fairly satisfactory manner.
5. Child continues to cry or to cling to mother, and cannot be persuaded to take the tests, even with mother present, or takes too few to justify a rating.

Negativism *

1. Child is entirely obedient and docile throughout tests; is willing at least to attempt whatever he is asked to do.
2. Child offers minor objections to some of the tests, but when urged and encouraged goes ahead with apparently undiminished effort.
3. Child requires much urging on any test which does not immediately appeal to his interest. May refuse flatly to try them at first, but objections can be overcome by subterfuge. Tests which arouse his interest are responded to readily.
4. Child shows a tendency to negativistic behavior on practically all the tests. Even tests which attract his interest are likely to be performed in the opposite way from that which he has been told. Subterfuge, bribery, or special firmness has to be used throughout in order to secure results.
5. Child refuses to take any of the tests, or takes too few to warrant a rating.

Distractibility

1. Child sits quietly during tests, gives good attention to directions throughout. Is not unduly distracted by outside stimuli, and does not interrupt test with irrelevant remarks.
2. Child sits quietly during tests, but is inclined to chatter on irrelevant subjects and is rather easily distracted by outside stimuli.
3. Child is somewhat restless, frequently climbing on table and attempting to handle material not then in use. Attention wanders easily but is also easily recalled.
4. Child is distinctly hyperactive, runs about room, snatches materials, inquires into everything he sees or hears. Attention can be held only for brief intervals, but by catching him "on the fly" he can be made to go through the tests.
5. Child shows extreme hyperactivity. Attention span so brief that he often loses track of what he is to do before completing a test. Results are too incomplete to warrant a rating.

* This may be an accompaniment of the behavior described under shyness, but it frequently occurs independently.

APPENDIX IV

Words with Frequencies of over 100 in the Present Study Listed in Order of Frequency

Word	Frequency	Word	Frequency	Word	Frequency
is	5164	be	578	make	283
the	3888	don't	576	just	281
a	3487	down	569	had	280
this	2867	like (adv.)	546	boy	275
I	2662	him	534	sheep	271
and	2633	over	505	big	265
to	2556	will	502	way	264
here	2405	know	501	pig	264
he	2269	uh-huh	487	am	263
they	2092	man	470	their	248
go	1944	can	452	well	239
one	1920	two	450	other	238
that	1821	out	445	how	237
there	1755	too	442	she	234
Indian	1656	at	436	eat	230
it	1282	has	430	but	229
of	1275	yes	426	something	229
these	1235	look	407	ride	224
are	1217	come	403	want	223
in	1154	no	399	could	203
up	1095	wagon	391	lot	203
got	1055	do	387	won't	197
horse	1043	then	386	broke, broken	197
have	933	see	371	anh-anh	195
them	901	thing	353	when	188
on	897	we	353	think	185
some	808	gun	345	were	184
shoot	776	my	341	girl	182
what	747	so	340	back	179
all	745	hm!	339	if	175
oh	715	was	334	kind	172
stand	711	more	314	suppose	171
little	682	because	313	didn't	170
another	672	play	312	try	168
now	661	where	312	dog	164
put	651	an	309	fall	164
cow	642	for	307	did	155
you	629	off	294	men	154
cowboy	627	would	290	guy	152
his	620	right	288	pull	152
tree	616	can't	288	use	151
with	615	take	284	school	151
get	599	buffalo	283	white	149

Word	Frequency	Word	Frequency	Word	Frequency
does	148	from	125	book	109
food	144	hand	125	brother	108
bow and arrow	139	mother	125	covered	105
home	139	saw	125	doesn't	105
guess	138	came	125	good	105
ain't	137	or	124	long	105
oxen	137	by	123	why	105
after	136	uh (er)	120	those	104
toy	135	animal	119	away	103
around	134	car	116	chief	103
people	133	me	116	her	103
time	132	run	116	kitten (kitty)	103
isn't	131	shot	115	baby	102
any	130	together	115	along	102
like (verb)	128	sometimes	114	fell	102
lay	126				

APPENDIX V

Number of Principal Coordinating and Subordinating Conjunctions Used by the 5½-Year Group

Conjunction	Twins			Singletons			Only Children			All		
	Boys	Girls	Both	Boys	Girls	Both	Boys	Girls	Both	Boys	Girls	Both
Coordinating Conjunctions												
And	191	202	316	123	220	343	74	141	215	311	563	874
But	10	13	23	26	32	58	3	24	27	39	69	108
Or, nor, either . . .	3	4	7	6	5	11	5	9	14	14	18	32
Neither	2	7	9	2	5	7	4	2	6	8	14	22
Subordinating Conjunctions												
If	10	7	17	7	11	18	6	8	14	23	26	49
Because	9	24	33	8	11	19	5	22	27	22	57	79
Though	6	4	10	11	14	25	7	8	15	24	26	50
Unless	0	0	0	0	0	0	0	0	0	0	0	0

APPENDIX VI

Number of Principal Coordinating and Subordinating Conjunctions Used by the 6½-Year Group

CONJUNCTION	TWINS			SINGLETONS			ONLY CHILDREN			ALL		
	Boys	Girls	Both	Boys	Girls	Both	Boys	Girls	Both	Boys	Girls	Both
Coordinating Conjunctions												
And	81	44	125	38	76	114	44	47	91	163	167	330
But	3	9	12	8	4	12	4	15	19	15	28	43
Or, nor, either	0	1	1	3	2	5	2	3	5	5	6	11
Neither	0	2	2	2	4	6	0	0	0	2	6	8
Subordinating Conjunctions												
If	2	1	3	5	6	11	4	7	11	11	14	25
Because	5	10	15	3	3	6	7	4	11	15	17	32
Though	4	2	6	5	1	6	8	6	14	17	9	26
Unless	0	0	0	0	0	0	0	0	0	0	0	0

APPENDIX VII

NUMBER OF PRINCIPAL COORDINATING AND SUBORDINATING CONJUNCTIONS USED BY THE 9½-YEAR GROUP

CONJUNCTION	TWINS			SINGLETONS			ONLY CHILDREN			ALL		
	Boys	Girls	Both	Boys	Girls	Both	Boys	Girls	Both	Boys	Girls	Both
Coordinating Conjunctions												
And	178	276	454	259	368	627	140	208	348	577	852	1429
But	20	3	23	13	18	31	13	11	24	46	32	78
Or, nor, either	11	8	19	32	18	50	3	11	14	46	37	83
Neither	1	1	2	2	2	4	1	0	1	4	3	7
Than	4	2	6	7	1	8	2	2	4	13	5	18
Subordinating Conjunctions												
If	20	9	29	22	26	48	12	12	24	54	47	101
Because	25	45	70	53	37	90	14	41	55	92	123	215
Though	4	2	6	3	5	8	1	3	4	8	10	18
Unless	0	0	0	1	0	1	0	0	0	1	0	1

APPENDIX VIII

SAMPLE RECORDS

For the convenience of persons who may be interested in the techniques of classification and scoring, three sample records, one for each age level studied, are here presented. The record selected was in each case the one nearest the mean length for the group which it represented. Remarks in brackets were made by the examiner.

J.G. Twin boy, age 5½ years. Occupational Group V. Time 5 minutes. IQ 89. Occasional substitution of *d* for *th*. Interest, shyness, and negativism 1; distractibility 2. Number of different words 110. Errors and slang 13.

No.	Remark	Function	Construction	Length in Words
1.	Where did — are these from Christmas? [Some of them came from Dayton's. You used to live in Minneapolis, so you know where Dayton's is.]	Question	Change of form	6
2.	Uh-huh.	Associated with conversation	Functionally complete	1
3.	Do you know where Cramer lives? [No]	Question	Complex sentence	6
4.	Well, he lives right by street light.	Associated with conversation	Simple sentence with phrase	7
5.	If you want to go over by Minneapolis, I might go with you and show you.	Associated with conversation	Elaborated sentence	16
6.	Is there Christmas trees in here?	Question	Simple sentence with phrase	6
7.	These good — new, aren't it?	Judgment	Fragmentary	5
8.	Is this a Christmas tree?	Question	Simple sentence	5
9.	Lot of 'em?	Question	Incomplete sentence	3
10.	I know where kindergarten is.	Judgment	Complex sentence	5
11.	Here's Indians riding on horses too.	Classification	Simple sentence with phrase	7
12.	And a black horsie and a man.	Classification	Functionally complete	7
13.	Gee, I like these.	Judgment	Simple sentence	4
14.	You should get up front.	Judgment	Simple sentence	5
15.	What this guy doing? [Shooting]	Question	Verb omitted	4
16.	Gosh!	Emotionally toned	Functionally complete	1

No.	Remark	Function	Construction	Length in Words
17.	I don't like mens that shoot.	Judgment	Complex sentence	6
18.	Do you?	Question	Functionally complete	2
19.	What are these made out of?	Question	Simple sentence with phrase	6
20.	Hey, something fell over.	Judgment	Simple sentence	4
21.	Didn't break.	Judgment	Subject omitted	2
22.	What is this?	Question	Simple sentence	3
23.	Pretty things.	Judgment	Functionally complete	2
24.	Hey, dis guy can wave his hand.	Judgment	Simple sentence	7
25.	Black horsie and a brown horsie.	Classification	Functionally complete	6
26.	Dey don't break, do dey?	Judgment	Simple sentence	5
27.	Where is it?	Question	Simple sentence	3
28.	Way over here.	Judgment	Fragmentary	3
29.	Went over here.	Judgment	Subject omitted	3
30.	Another little donkey.	Classification	Functionally complete	3
31.	Well, that drops all the time.	Judgment	Simple sentence	6
32.	I have to ——	Judgment	Fragmentary	3
33.	It wiggles, maybe that's why it drops.	Judgment	Conjunction omitted	8
34.	Say, this hand is broke off.	Part-whole	Simple sentence	6
35.	Hanh?	Question	Functionally complete	1
36.	It's too hard, I think.	Judgment	Complex sentence	6
37.	Gosh, there's good stuff around here.	Judgment	Simple sentence with phrase	7
38.	You have to stand them up.	Judgment	Simple sentence	6
39.	They have to lay down and go sleep now.	Judgment	Simple sentence with phrase	9
40.	There's mans around there.	Naming	Simple sentence with phrase	5
41.	And trees.	Naming	Functionally complete	2
42.	And horses, and man, and guns.	Naming	Functionally complete	6
43.	And trees.	Naming	Functionally complete	1
44.	Horses.	Naming	Functionally complete	1
45.	Trees.	Naming	Functionally complete	2
46.	Christmas trees.	Naming	Functionally complete	2
47.	Anudder tree.	Classification	Functionally complete	2
48.	And horses again.	Classification	Functionally complete	3
49.	Horses again.	Classification	Functionally complete	2
50.	Have you got — have you got a little boy?	Question	Simple sentence	9

D. K. Only girl, aged 6½ years. Occupational Group III. Time 20 minutes. IQ 121. All ratings 1. Number of different words 110. Errors and slang 13.

1.	Horse.	Naming	Functionally complete	1
2.	Tee-hee (laughing), cute!	Emotionally toned	Functionally complete	2
3.	Tee-hee, little lambs!	Classification	Functionally complete	3

No.	Remark	Function	Construction	Length in Words
4.	There!	Emotionally toned	Functionally complete	1
5.	They're sitting there watching the car go by.	Associated with situation	Elaborated sentence	9
6.	There's a place to put on.	Classification	Complex sentence	7
7.	No, not that.	Judgment	Functionally complete	3
8.	They're trucking by.	Associated with situation	Simple sentence	4
9.	The cow don't — oh!	Judgment	Incomplete	4
10.	I thought it could be sitting in the window, but it can't.	Judgment	Elaborated sentence	12
11.	I'm going to make a parade.	Associated with situation	Simple sentence	7
12.	He's turning the corner.	Associated with situation	Simple sentence	5
13.	There!	Emotionally toned	Functionally complete	1
14.	I'm going to make something else now.	Associated with situation	Simple sentence	8
15.	Won't stand up. [Perhaps you can bend its legs a little.]	Judgment	Subject omitted	3
16.	Yeah.	Associated with conversation	Functionally complete	1
17.	Then it'll stand up.	Judgment	Simple sentence	5
18.	Shooting an arrow.	Associated with situation	Subject, verb omitted	3
19.	What's *he* doing? [He has a tomahawk.]	Question	Simple sentence	4
20.	Looks like an axe.	Associated with conversation	Subject omitted	4
21.	Let's see — wonder who — oh, this can be leading the parade.	Judgment	Change of form	11
22.	Where's the horse that *he* drives?	Question	Complex sentence	7
23.	Oh, I'll find something. [You might find something in the other box.]	Associated with situation	Simple sentence	5
24.	All right, put these away now.	Associated with conversation	Subject, verb omitted	5
25.	That won't fit in.	Judgment	Simple sentence	4
26.	Is there a cover? [Yes.]	Question	Simple sentence	4
27.	Where's it?	Question	Simple sentence	3
28.	Let's see, I don't think I can get it off.	Judgment	Complex sentence	10
29.	Oh yes, I can.	Judgment	Functionally complete	4
30.	Boy! (seeing covered wagon).	Emotionally toned	Functionally complete	1
31.	There's nice ones in here.	Judgment	Simple sentence with phrase	6

No.	Remark	Function	Construction	Length in Words
32.	Oh boy, I'm going to find something keen.	Associated with situation	Simple sentence	8
33.	There's just enough.	Quantitative discrimination	Simple sentence	4
34.	I'm going to put that one on there instead.	Associated with situation	Simple sentence with phrase	10
35.	There, now they're going.	Associated with situation	Simple sentence with phrase	5
36.	I'm going to change them around a different way.	Associated with situation	Simple sentence	· 10
37.	There!	Emotionally toned	Functionally complete	1
38.	They're going to fall off.	Associated with situation	Simple sentence	, 6
39.	I've seen one of these at somebody else's house.	Associated with situation	Elaborated sentence	10
40.	I went over to a girl's house and I seen one of them, but in the middle there was a different thing.	Associated with situation	Elaborated sentence	22
41.	There!	Emotionally toned	Functionally complete	1
42.	Boy, it still looks pretty. [You can hitch two pairs of oxen together.]	**Judgment**	Simple sentence	5
43.	Sure, I just seen that.	Associated with conversation	Simple sentence	5
44.	This falls out.	Judgment	Simple sentence	3
45.	Can't use them. [That's what we would have to do if the wagons were stuck in the mud.]	Judgment	Subject omitted	3
46.	Yeah.	Associated with conversation	Functionally complete	1
47.	Going to be a big long one this time.	Judgment	Subject, verb omitted	9
48.	Tee-hee! (laughs as examiner sets out Indians).	Emotionally toned	Functionally complete	1
49.	Well, I'll fix them a different way.	Associated with conversation	Simple sentence	8
50.	There!	Emotionally toned	Functionally complete	1

W. G. Singleton boy, age 9½ years. Occupational Group III. Time 16 minutes. IQ 119. All ratings 1. Number of different words 152. Errors and slang 18.

1.	Like this?	Question	Functionally complete	2
2.	Won't be able to use all of these.	Judgment	Subject omitted	8
3.	That one doesn't stand so well.	Judgment	Simple sentence	6

No.	Remark	Function	Construction	Length in Words
4.	Uh-huh.	Associated with conversation	Functionally complete	1
5.	Put these over here.	Judgment	Subject omitted	4
6.	This isn't right.	Judgment	Simple sentence	3
7.	This one doesn't stand so good, on his feet.	Judgment	Simple sentence with phrase	9
8.	This here hand moves, huh?	Associated with situation	Simple sentence	5
9.	This one has, too.	Associated with conversation	Simple sentence	4
10.	Let's see.	Monologue	Functionally complete	2
11.	He's s'posed to be shooting at Indians.	Judgment	Elaborated	8
12.	This one hasn't lost his.	Associated with conversation	Simple sentence	5
13.	This arm must have been shot off.	Part-whole	Simple sentence	7
14.	S'pose he — this un ——	Judgment	Fragmentary	4
15.	Too bad there isn't some grass around here.	Judgment	Subject, verb omitted	8
16.	You should get some of the stuff that looks something like it.	Associated with conversation	Elaborated sentence	12
17.	That one s'pose you had drinking.	Associated with conversation	Subject omitted	6
18.	That there one is hiding behind the bushes.	Associated with situation	Simple sentence with phrase	8
	[When did they use wagons like these?]			
19.	Oh — er — about thirty or forty years ago.	Answer	Functionally complete	8
20.	Fifty, somep'n like that.	Associated with situation	Fragmentary	4
	[Why don't we use them now?]			
21.	We got automobiles and that.	Answer	Simple sentence	5
	[What did they use them for?]			
22.	Well, to travel —	Answer	Functionally complete	3
23.	Through mountains.	Associated with situation	Functionally complete	2
	[Why did a number of wagons go along together?]			
24.	Well, if they had war, and some Indians started attackting them they'd have a lot of 'em.	Answer	Elaborated sentence	18
25.	Just one, they get 'em.	Associated with situation	Fragmentary	5
26.	Have to have that walking on the side.	Judgment	Subject omitted	8
	[Did they use these extra oxen?]			

No.	Remark	Function	Construction	Length in Words
27.	Sure.	Answer	Functionally complete	1
28.	If they happened to get stuck and that, and they'd have to have some help. [Why did they use oxen instead of horses?]	Associated with situation	Changed form	16
29.	Well, oxens is stronger than they, and they can pull better. [What did they use horses for?]	Answer	Compound sentence	11
30.	Used their horses for riding. [Why did the Indians attack them?]	Answer	Subject omitted	5
31.	Well, to get things and rob. [What did they have that the Indians wanted?]	Answer	Functionally complete	6
32.	Guns, and then skins.	Answer	Functionally complete	4
33.	And skins.	Associated with conversation	Functionally complete	2
34.	To kill and —	Answer	Fragmentary	3
35.	Er — buffalo, they shot. [Why did the Indians want horses?]	Associated with situation	Simple sentence	4
36.	Well, they could go faster than oxen, and they could kill the buffaloes lots easier. [What is he shooting at?]	Answer	Compound sentence	15
37.	Well, he's aiming for the Indians. [Who is this?]	Answer	Simple sentence with phrase	7
38.	A soldier, guard.	Answer	Functionally complete	3
39.	This here is, too. [Why did they have scouts along?]	Classification	Simple sentence	4
40.	To keep guard and if anything happened to get 'tackt and that, they'd —	Answer	Incomplete	14
41.	Oh. [Where were they going in the wagons?]	Answer	Functionally complete	1
42.	Sometimes they were going to get land and that. [What kind of animal would they see?]	Answer	Complex sentence	9
43.	Wild.	Answer	Functionally complete	1
44.	They had pretty many of them too.	Associated with conversation	Simple sentence with phrase	7
45.	They could lead the way and —	Associated with conversation	Incomplete	6

No.	Remark	Function	Construction	Length in Words
46.	And they'd know just about the Indian yells and the fire and that.	Associated with situation	Simple sentence with phrase	14
47.	If they — down cliffs. [Do you know the name of any scouts?]	Associated with conversation	Fragmentary	4
48.	I don't know — Buffalo Bill, I know he was a soldier in — er — Custer.	Answer	Changed form	14
49.	And that Custer, he had a little army, and they'd fight Indians.	Associated with situation	Compound sentence	13
50.	Let's see, Buffalo Bill was a pony express rider too.	Associated with situation	Simple sentence	10

BIBLIOGRAPHY

- 1. ADAMS, S. Study of the growth of language between two and four years. Journal of Juvenile Research, 16:269–77 (1932).
- 2. ANDERSON, JOHN E. An evaluation of various indices of language development. Child Development, 8:62–68 (1937).
3. ARTHUR, G. The relation of IQ to position in family. Journal of Educational Psychology, 17:541–50 (1926).
4. AVERILL, L. A., and A. D. MUELLER. Physical and mental measurements of fraternal twins. Pedagogical Seminary and Journal of Genetic Psychology, 32:612–27 (1925).
5. BAKWIN, R. M. Similarities and differences in identical twins. Pedagogical Seminary and Journal of Genetic Psychology, 38:373–97 (1930).
6. BAUER, N. New Orleans public school spelling list. F. F. Hansell and Bros., New Orleans, 1916.
- 7. BECK, R. L. A natural test of English usage. Journal of Experimental Education, 1:280–86 (1932).
- 8. BETZNER, JEAN. Content and form of original compositions dictated by children from five to eight years of age (Teachers College Contributions to Education, No. 442). New York, 1930. 53 pp.
9. BLANTON, M., and S. BLANTON. Speech training for children. Century Co., New York, 1924. xv + 261 pp.
- 10. BLANTON, S. A survey of speech defectives. Journal of Educational Psychology, 7:580–85 (1916).
11. BLATZ, W. E., and E. A. BOTT. Studies in mental hygiene of children. I. Behavior of public school children: a description of method. Pedagogical Seminary and Journal of Genetic Psychology, 34:552–82 (1927).
12. BLOCH, O. La phrase dans le langage de l'enfant. Journal de psychologie, 21:18–43 (1924).
13. ————. Le langage d'action dans les premières stades du langage de l'enfant. Journal de psychologie, 20:670–74 (1923).
14. BOHANNON, E. W. The only child in the family. Pedagogical Seminary, 5:475–96 (1898).
15. ————. Peculiar and exceptional children. Pedagogical Seminary, 4:3–60 (1896).
16. BOYD, W. The beginning of syntactical speech: a study in child linguistics. Child Study, 6:21–24, 47–51 (1913).
17. ————. The development of sentence structure in childhood. British Journal of Psychology, 17:181–91 (1926–27).
18. BRIDGES, K. M. B. Occupational interests of three-year-old children. Pedagogical Seminary and Journal of Genetic Psychology, 34:415–23 (1927).
19. BURKS, B., and R. S. TOLMAN. Is mental resemblance related to physical resemblances in sibling pairs? Pedagogical Seminary and Journal of Genetic Psychology, 40:3–15 (1932).
20. CAMPBELL, A. A. The personality adjustments of only children. Psychological Bulletin, 31:193–203 (1934).
21. CARRELL, J. A. Speech defects (Child Development Abstracts, Vol. VI, No. 838). 1933. Mimeographed.

22. CHAPMAN, J. C., and D. M. WIGGINS. Relation of family size to intelligence of offspring and socio-economic status of family. Pedagogical Seminary and Journal of Genetic Psychology, 32:414–21 (1925).

23. CHARTERS, W. W., and E. MILLER. A course of study in grammar based upon the grammatical errors of school children of Kansas City, Missouri (University of Missouri Bulletin, Vol. XVI, No. 2). 1915. 45 pp.

24. COMMINS, W. D. The intelligence of the later born. School and Society, 25:488–89 (1927).

25. CONRADI, E. The psychology and pathology of speech development in children. Pedagogical Seminary, 11:328–80 (1904).

26. ———. Speech development and intellectual progress. Journal of Educational Psychology, 3:35–38 (1912).

27. COOK, W. A., and M. V. O'SHEA. The child and his spelling. Bobbs-Merrill and Co., Indianapolis, 1914. vi + 282 pp.

28. DAHLBERG, G. Twin births and twins from a hereditary point of view. Tidens Tryckeri, Stockholm, 1926. 296 pp.

29. DAVID, D. The development of language habits. Journal of Educational Method, 5:155–60 (1925).

30. DAVIS, E. A. The form and function of children's questions. Child Development, 3:57–74 (1932).

31. DAY, ELLA J. The development of language in twins. Child Development, 3:179–99, 298–316 (1932).

32. DEWEY, G. Relative frequency of English speech sounds. Harvard University Press, Cambridge, 1923. xii + 148 pp.

33. DOLCH, E. W. Combined word studies. Journal of Educational Research, 17:11–19 (1928).

34. ———. Grade vocabularies. Journal of Educational Research, 16:16–26 (1927).

35. FENTON, N. The only child. Pedagogical Seminary and Journal of Genetic Psychology, 35:546–56 (1928).

36. FISHER, M. S. Language patterns of preschool children. Journal of Experimental Education, 1:70–85 (1932).

37. FRIEDJUNG, J. Die Pathologie des einzigen Kindes. Wiener klinesche Wochenschrift, 24:42 (1911).

38. GARRETT, H. E. Statistics in psychology and education. Longmans, Green and Co., New York, 1926. xiii + 317 pp.

39. GATES, A. I. Construction of a reading vocabulary for primary grades. Teachers College Record, 27:625–42 (1926).

40. GESELL, A., and E. LORD. A psychological comparison of nursery school children from homes of low and high economic status. Pedagogical Seminary and Journal of Genetic Psychology, 34:339–56 (1927).

41. GOODENOUGH, FLORENCE L. Anger in young children (University of Minnesota Institute of Child Welfare Monograph No. 9). University of Minnesota Press, 1931. xiii + 278 pp.

42. ———. The emotional behavior of young children during mental tests. Journal of Juvenile Research, 13:204–19 (1929).

43. ———. Interrelationships in the behavior of young children. Child Development, 1:29–47 (1930).

44. ———, and A. M. LEAHY. The effect of certain family relationships upon the development of personality. Pedagogical Seminary and Journal of Genetic Psychology, 34:45–71 (1927).

45. GUILER, W. S. Analysis of children's writings as a basis for instruction in English. Journal of Educational Method, 5:258–64 (1926).

46. ———. Improving ability in verb usage. Elementary School Journal, 31:524–30 (1930–31).

47. GUILFORD, R. B., and D. A. WORCESTER. Only and non-only children. Pedagogical Seminary and Journal of Genetic Psychology, 38: 411–26 (1930).
48. GUILLAUME, P. Les débuts de la phrase dans le langage de l'enfant. Journal de psychologie, 24:1–25 (1927).
49. HAWTHORNE, J. W. An attempt to measure certain phases of speech. Pedagogical Seminary and Journal of Genetic Psychology, 10:399–414 (1934).
50. HIRSCH, N. D. M. An experimental study upon 300 school children over a six-year-period (Genetic Psychology Monographs, Vol. VII, No. 6). 1930. 62 pp.
51. ————. Twins: heredity and environment. Harvard University Press, Cambridge, 1930. 159 pp.
52. HOOKER, H. F. A study of the only child at school. Pedagogical Seminary and Journal of Genetic Psychology, 39:122–26 (1931). .
53. HORN, E. The commonest words in the spoken vocabulary of children up to and including six years of age. Yearbook of the National Society for the Study of Education, 1925, Part I, pp. 185–99.
54. HORN, M. D. The 1,003 words most frequently used by kindergarten children. Childhood Education, 3:118–22 (1926–27).
55. HOWARD, RUTH. A developmental study of triplets. Unpublished Ph.D. dissertation, University of Minnesota, 1934. xxiii + 312 pp.
56. HSIAO, H. H. The status of the first-born with special reference to intelligence (Genetic Psychology Monographs, Vol. IX, Nos. 1 and 2). 1931.
57. HUNT, E. B. The genetic primacy of hedonic terms. American Journal of Psychology, 44:369–70 (1932).
58. INTERNATIONAL KINDERGARTEN UNION. A study of the vocabulary of children before entering the first grade. Williams and Wilkins, Baltimore, 1928. 36 pp.
59. ISAACS, SUSAN. Intellectual growth in young children. Harcourt, Brace and Co., New York, 1930. xi + 370 pp.
60. JESPERSON, O. Language, its nature, development, and origin. Allen and Unwin, London, 1922. 448 pp.
61. JOHNSON, R. I. The persistency of error in English compositions. School Review, 25:555–80 (1917).
62. JONES, H. E. Order of birth in relation to the development of the child. Handbook of child psychology, pp. 204–41. Clark University Press, Worcester, Massachusetts, 1931.
63. ————, and P. T. WILSON. Reputation differences in like-sexed twins. Journal of Experimental Education, 1:86–91 (1932–33).
64. JONES, W. F. A concrete investigation of the material of English spelling. University of South Dakota, Vermilion, 1914. 29 pp.
65. KATZ, D., and R. KATZ. Gespräche mit Kindern (Untersuchungen zur Social-Psychologie und Pädagogik). Springer, Berlin, 1927. vi + 299 pp.
66. KIRKPATRICK, E. A. Fundamentals of child study. Macmillan Co., New York, 1903. 385 pp.
67. ————. The number of words in ordinary vocabularies. Science, 18:107–08 (1891).
68. KOLRAUSCHE, E. Jugendspiele und Einzelsöhne. Zeitschrift für Schulegesundheitspflege, 4:178 (1891).
69. LaBRANT, L. Studies of certain language developments of children in grades four to twelve inclusive (Genetic Psychology Monographs, Vol. XIV, No. 5). 1933.
70. LAUTERBACH, C. E. Studies in twin resemblance. Genetics, 10:525–68 (1925).

71. LEHMAN, H. C., and P. A. WITTY. The psychology of play activities. Barnes, New York, 1927. xviii + 242 pp.

72. LENTZ, T. Relation of IQ to size of family. Journal of Educational Psychology, 18:486–96 (1927).

73. LEONARD, S. A., and H. Y. MOFFELT. Current definition of levels in English usage. English Journal, 16:349–59 (1927).

74. LEVY, D. M. The relation of maternal overprotection to school grades and intelligence tests. American Journal of Orthopsychiatry, 3:26–34 (1933).

75. LIMA, M. Speech defects in children. Mental Hygiene, 11:795–803 (1927).

76. LOOFT, C. Mental development of twins. Acta Paediatrica, 12:41 (1931). Reviewed in Child Development Abstracts, 2:163 (1933). Mimeographed.

77. LYMAN, R. L. Fluency, accuracy, and general excellence in English composition. School Review, 26:85–100 (1918).

78. ————. Summary of investigations relating to grammar, language, and composition (University of Chicago Supplementary Education Monograph No. 36). University of Chicago Press, 1929. 302 pp.

79. MCCARTHY, DOROTHEA. A comparison of children's language in different situations and its relation to personality traits. Pedagogical Seminary and Journal of Genetic Psychology, 36:583–91 (1929).

80. ————. Language development of the preschool child (University of Minnesota Institute of Child Welfare Monograph No. 4). University of Minnesota Press, 1930. xiii + 174 pp.

81. MCCONNON, K. The situation factor in the language responses of nursery school children. Unpublished Ph.D. dissertation, University of Minnesota, 1935. v + 192 pp.

82. MAJOR, D. R. First steps in mental growth: a series of studies in the psychology of infancy. Macmillan Co., New York, 1906. xiv + 360 pp.

83. MALLER, J. B. Size of family and personality of offspring. Journal of Social Psychology, 2:3–27 (1931).

84. MARKEY, J. F. The symbolic process. Harcourt, Brace and Co., New York, 1928. ix + 142 pp.

85. MARSTON, L. R. The emotions of young children (University of Iowa Studies in Child Welfare, Vol. III, No. 3). University of Iowa, 1925. 99 pp.

86. MELTZER, H. Talkativeness in stuttering children. Pedagogical Seminary and Journal of Genetic Psychology, 46:371–90 (1935).

87. MERRIMAN, C. The intellectual resemblance of twins (Psychological Monographs, Vol. 33, No. 5). 1924. 58 pp.

88. MOORE, K. C. The mental development of a child (Psychological Review Monographs, Supplement I, No. 3). 1896. 150 pp.

89. MORRISON, E. E. Speech defects in young children. Psychological Clinic, 8:138–42 (1914).

90. MURRAY, ELWOOD. The disintegration of breathing and eye movements of stutterers during silent reading and reasoning. Unpublished thesis, University of Iowa, 1931. Discussed in L. E. Travis, Speech pathology. Appleton and Co., New York, 1931.

91. NEWMAN, H. H. Mental and physical traits of identical twins reared apart. Journal of Heredity, 20:49–64, 97–104, 153–66 (1929); 23:2–18 (1932).

92. NICE, M. M. Analysis of conversation of children and adults. Child Development, 3:240–46 (1932).

93. ————. A child's attainment of the sentence. Pedagogical Seminary and Journal of Genetic Psychology, 42:216–24 (1933).

94. ————. Length of sentences as a criterion of a child's progress in speech. Journal of Educational Psychology, 16:370–79 (1925).

95. ————. On the size of vocabularies. American Speech, 2:1–7 (1926).

96. ————. Speech development of a child from eighteen months to six years. Pedagogical Seminary, 24:204–43 (1917).

97. OGBURN, WILLIAM F. The family and its functions, in Recent Social Trends, Vol. I. McGraw-Hill Co., New York, 1933.

98. OGDEN, C. K. Basic English. K. Paul, Trench, Trubner, and Co., London, 1933. 95 pp.

99. O'SHEA, M. V. Linguistic development and education. Macmillan, New York, 1907. xviii + 347 pp.

100. PAYNE, C. S. The mispronunciation of words. Pedagogical Seminary and Journal of Genetic Psychology, 38:427–44 (1930).

101. PEARSON, H. C., and H. SUZZALLO. Essentials of spelling. American Book Company, New York, 1919. xcii + 196 pp.

102. PIAGET, JEAN. The language and thought of the child. Harcourt, Brace and Co., New York, 1926. xxiii + 246 pp.

103. PILLSBURY, W. B., and C. L. MEADER. The psychology of language. Appleton, New York, 1928. vii + 306 pp.

104. PRESCOTT, D. A. Le vocabulaire des enfants des écoles primaires de Genève. Archives de psychologie, 21:225–61 (1929).

105. PREYER, W. The mind of the child. Part II of The development of the intellect (translated by H. W. Brown). Appleton, New York, 1889. xli + 317 pp.

106. RANDOLPH, E. D. Conventional aversions versus fundamental errors in spoken English. Pedagogical Seminary, 24:318–36 (1917).

107. REMER, L. M. Handicaps of school entrants. University of Iowa Studies in Child Welfare, Vol. VI, pp. 195–207. University of Iowa, 1932.

108. REXROAD, C. N. Recent studies of twin resemblance. Psychological Bulletin, 29:204–17 (1932).

109. ROOT, A. R. A survey of speech defectives in the public elementary schools of South Dakota. Elementary School Journal, 26:531–41 (1926).

110. ROSE, H. N. A thesaurus of slang. Macmillan Co., New York, 1934. 120 pp.

111. RUGG, H., L. KRUEGER, and A. SONDERGAARD. Studies in child personality. I. A study of the language of kindergarten children. Journal of Educational Psychology, 20:1–18 (1929).

112. SANCHEZ, G. I. Implications of a basal vocabulary to measurement of ability of bilingual children. Journal of Social Psychology, 5:395–402 (1934).

113. SANGREN, P. V. Comparative validity of primary intelligence tests. Journal of Applied Psychology, 13:394–412 (1929).

114. SCHNECK, M. M. Measurement of verbal and numerical abilities (Archives of Psychology, Vol. XVII, No. 107). 1929. 49 pp.

115. SCHWESINGER, G. C. Slang as an indication of character. Journal of Applied Psychology, 10:245–63 (1926).

116. SEARS, I., and A. DIEBEL. Study of common mistakes in pupils' oral English. Elementary School Journal, 17:44–54 (1916).

117. SECHRIST, F. K. Psychology of unconventional language. Pedagogical Seminary, 2:413–59 (1913).

118. SHAMBAUGH, C. G., and O. L. SHAMBAUGH. An association study of vocabularies of grade children. Journal of Educational Research, 18:40–47 (1928).

119. SKALET, MAGDA. The play equipment of two-, three-, and four-year-old children. Unpublished M.A. thesis, University of Minnesota, 1928. 180 pp.

120. SMITH, M. E. Grammatical errors in the speech of preschool children. Child Development, 4:182–90 (1933).

121. ————. The influence of age, sex, and situation on the frequency, form,

and function of questions asked by preschool children. Child Development, 4:201–13 (1933).

122. ————. An investigation of the development of the sentence and the extent of vocabulary in young children (University of Iowa Studies in Child Welfare, Vol. III, No. 5). University of Iowa, 1926. 92 pp.

123. ————. The preschool child's use of criticism. Child Development, 3:134–41 (1932).

124. ————. A study of five bilingual children from the same family. Child Development, 2:184–87 (1931).

125. ————. A study of some factors influencing the development of the sentence in preschool children. Pedagogical Seminary and Journal of Genetic Psychology, 46:182–212 (1935).

126. ————. A study of the speech of eight bilingual children of the same family. Child Development, 6:19–25 (1935).

127. SOMMERS, A. T. The effect of group training upon the correction of articulatory defects in preschool children. Child Development, 3:91–103 (1932).

128. SPRINGOB, J. R. Factors influencing the incidence of articulatory speech defects in preschool children. Unpublished M.A. thesis, University of Minnesota, 1930. 99 pp.

129. STALNAKER, E. The language of preschool children. Child Development, 4:229–36 (1933).

130. STECKEL, M. L. Intelligence and birth order in family. Journal of Social Psychology, 1:329–44 (1930).

131. STERN, W. Psychology of early childhood, up to the sixth year of age. Holt and Co., New York, 1924. 557 pp.

132. STEVENSON, A. The speech of children. Science, 21:18–20 (1893).

133. STINCHFIELD, S. M. The psychology of speech. Expression Co., Boston, 1928. ix + 331 pp.

134. STODDARD, G. D., and BETH WELLMAN. Child psychology. Macmillan Co., New York, 1934. xii + 419 pp.

135. STORMZAND, M. J., and M. V. O'SHEA. How much English grammar? Warwick and York, Baltimore, 1924. vii + 224 pp.

136. SUNNE, DAGNY. The effect of locality on language errors. Journal of Educational Research, 8:239–51 (1933).

137. SUTHERLAND, H. E. G., and G. H. THOMPSON. The correlation between intelligence and size of family. British Journal of Psychology, 17:81–92 (1926).

138. TIDYMAN, W. F. A survey of writing vocabularies of public school children in Connecticut (United States Bureau of Education, Teacher's Leaflet No. 15). Government Printing Office, Washington, D.C., November, 1921.

139. ————. The teaching of spelling. World Book Co., Yonkers-on-Hudson, New York, 1922. 178 pp.

140. THORNDIKE, E. L. Teacher's word book. Teachers College, New York, 1921. vi + 134 pp.

141. THURSTONE, L. L., and R. L. JENKINS. Birth order and intelligence. Journal of Educational Psychology, 20:641–51 (1929).

142. TOWN, C. H. An analytic study of a group of five- to six-year-old children (University of Iowa Studies in Child Welfare, Vol. I, No. 4). University of Iowa, 1925. 87 pp.

143. ————. Language development in 285 idiots and imbeciles. Psychological Clinic, 6:229–35 (1912–13).

144. TRACY, F. The language of childhood. American Journal of Psychology, 6:107–38 (1893). Also published in the Psychology of childhood, 7th edition, pp. 118–65. Heath, Boston, 1909.

145. VASEY, F. T. Vocabularies of grammar school children. Journal of Educational Psychology, 10:104–07 (1919).

146. VYGOTSKY, L. S., and A. R. LURIA. The function and fate of egocentric speech. Proceedings and Papers of the Ninth International Congress of Psychologists, 1929, pp. 464–65. 1930.

147. WALLIN, J. E. W. A census of speech defectives among 89,057 public school pupils. School and Society, 3:213–16 (1916).

148. ————. Report on speech defects in St. Louis public schools. Board of Education, St. Louis, 1915, 1916.

149. WELLMAN, BETH, I. CASE, I. MENGERT, and D. BRADBURY. Speech sounds of young children (University of Iowa Studies in Child Welfare, Vol. V, No. 2). University of Iowa, 1931. 82 pp.

150. WHEELER, H. E., and E. HOWELL. A first-grade vocabulary study. Elementary School Journal, 31:52–60 (1930).

151. WILE, I., and E. NOETZEL. A study of birth order and behavior. Journal of Social Psychology, 2:52–71 (1931).

152. WILLIAMS, H. M. An analytical study of expressive use of language at the preschool level (Child Development Abstracts, Vol. VII, No. 1182). 1933. Mimeographed.

153. ————. Some problems of sampling in vocabulary tests. Journal of Experimental Education, 1:131–33 (1932–33).

154. WINGFIELD, A. H. Twins and orphans: the inheritance of intelligence. Dent, London, 1928. 127 pp.

155. WILSON, G. M. Errors in language of grade pupils. Educator, December, 1909.

156. ————. Language error tests. Journal of Educational Psychology, 13:341–49 (1922).

157. ————. Locating the language errors of school children. Elementary School Journal, 21:290–96 (1920).

158. WILSON, M. A. Persistence of error in use of the English language by school children. Unpublished M.A. thesis, University of Southern California, 1923.

159. WILSON, P. T., and H. E. JONES. Left-handedness in twins. Journal of Genetics, 17:560–71 (1932).

160. WOODCOCK, L. P. When children first say why, because, if (Cooperating School Pamphlets No. 7). Bureau of Educational Experiments, 1934.

161. WORCESTER, D. A. Schoolroom attitudes and achievements of only children. Pedagogical Seminary and Journal of Genetic Psychology, 38:475–80 (1930).

162. ZIPF, G. K. The psychobiology of language. Houghton Mifflin, Boston, 1935. ix + 336 pp.

163. ZYVE, C. I. Conversation among children. Teachers College Record, 29:46–61 (1927).

INDEX

Adults, use of subordinate clauses, 87–90, 92; errors, 100; use of infinitives, 94; language, 84, 133

Age, chronological, and number of answers, 61–71, 81, 132–33; and use of articles, 118, 121, 132, conjunctions, 119–21, 132, 144–46, pronouns, 117, 132, slang, 119–21, 132; improvement in articulation with, 33–35, 132; and number of subordinate clauses, 89–94, 132; and index of subordination, 88, 91, 132; and number of questions, 71–72, 132; and egocentric remarks, 77, 133; and emotionally toned remarks, 132; and one-word remarks, 60, 132–33; increase in sentence length with, 44, 47–54, 132; and variability in sentence length, 55–59, 132; and number of different words, 112, 120, 132. *See also* Errors; Sentences; Structure

Anderson, John E., 88

Answers, 66–81 *passim*; acquiescence, 71; affirmation and denial, 70–71; analysis, 69–71; number of one-word, 79, 81; percentage in twins, singletons, and only children, 135; "yes" and "no," 70–71, 80

Arthur, G., 6

Articles, definite and indefinite, 83, 115–16, 121, 132

Articulation, 4, 7; effect on personality and behavior, 38–42; previous investigations, 28–31; method of measuring, 31–32; and naming, 75; percentage of subjects perfect, 33–35; in like- and unlike-sex twins, 123, 126–27, 130

Bakwin, R. M., 4
Bateman, W. G., 108
Betzner, J., 4
Bilingualism, 4, 37
Blanton, S., 5
Blatz, W. E., 5
Bloch, O., 87, 106
Bohannon, E. W., 5
Bott, E. A., 5
Boyd, W., 87, 94
Burks, B. S., 4

Calculations, questions of, 73

Campbell, A. A., 6

Carrell, J. A., 30

Cause, adverbial clauses of, 87, 93, 103; questions of, 73

Charters, W. W., 103

Classification, 64, 75–76; questions of, 73

Clause, adjectival, use, 83, 91, importance, 91–94; adverbial, use, 83, importance, 92, 103, distribution, 94; noun, use, 82–83, 93, 103; in defective speakers, 41; subordinate, 82–95, 132–35; types of, variations with age, importance, 91–94; as unit of measurement, 4, 28

Commins, W. D., 5

Comparison, 64, 67, 78; of adjectives, errors in, 101–02; adverbial clauses of, 93; of groups, on basis of age, 132–33, parental occupation, 134, sex, 133–34, sibling relationship, 135–37; of like- and unlike-sex twins, 123, 126–29; of twins with unrelated pairs, 122–25

Concession, adverbial clauses of, 93

Condition, adverbial clauses of, 87, 93, 104

Conjunctions, 109; errors in use, 102; omission, 83, 87, 91, 116; order of appearance, 87–88. *See also* Age, and use of conjunctions

Conradi, E., 30

Conversation, 76; of young children, 87, 106, 110; and parental occupation, 67; remarks associated with, 65–67, 76–77, 80–81; limited by toys, 21; variation in, 23. *See also* Adults

Criticism, 67. *See also* Judgment

Dahlberg, G., 122

Davis, E. A., 43, 59, 61n, 72, 134n

Day, E. J., 3, 4, 7, 11, 19–22, 26, 29, 33, 41, 43, 44, 49–51, 67, 75, 80, 84–85, 87, 106, 109, 112–13, 122, 128, 131, 137

Definition, 65, 67

Description, 76

Dewey, G., 107, 112

Distractibility, in defective speakers, 88; and length of remarks, 47, 62; ratings for, 24–25